HOW GOOD IS YOUR CHESS?

DANIEL KING
International Grandmaster

DOVER PUBLICATIONS, INC.
Mineola, New York

Bibliographical Note

This Dover edition, first published in 2003, is an unabridged and slightly corrected republication of the work originally published by Cadogan Chess Books, London, in 1993.

Library of Congress Cataloging-in-Publication Data

King, Daniel.
    How good is your chess? / Daniel King.
        p. cm.
    Originally published: London : Cadogan Chess Books, 1993.
    ISBN 0-486-42780-3 (pbk.)
      1. Chess problems—Collections of games. I. Title.

GV1451 .K58 2003
794.1'2—dc21   2002041303

Manufactured in the United States of America
Dover Publications, Inc., 31 East 2nd Street, Mineola, N.Y. 11501

Contents

Introduction

Every chessplayer, no matter what their strength, wishes to improve their play — but how should one go about doing this? Playing as much as possible is bound to help, but at some point a barrier is reached, and that is when it is necessary to sit down at home with your chessboard, a pile of dog-eared scoresheets from your last tournament on the table next to you, and try to examine exactly what is going wrong. Going over one's own games is important, but I find that it is often the discovery of new ideas which rekindles my enthusiasm for the game.

I suspect that if chessplayers do any 'homework' it is the openings on which they concentrate. There is a great danger with this. Many books simply give lines of play without a great deal of explanation, and then break off just when the struggle is hotting up, ending with an assessment such as 'equal' or 'slight advantage to White'. What good does that do us? It is necessary to understand the fundamentals of the position in order to know how to proceed. And who knows, perhaps someone in the next Russian junior championships will find a devastating improvement overturning the assessment of the whole variation? Studying openings is, at best, beneficial only in the short term. It is much better to look at complete games in order to get an idea of the overall strategy in different kinds of positions.

This book will not only help you to judge your standard of play, but by giving you the chance to work out and study the plans and ideas of some of the world's top players, should also help you to improve your game. I have selected twenty games. In each game, beginning after the first diagram, you will have to predict the moves of one of the players, so for instance in game 1, you will be guessing all the Black moves; and in game 2 the White moves. Cover the page with a card or sheet of paper, lowering it a line at a time so that you don't see the moves ahead. If you are predicting Black's moves, then you should stop after you see a White move and try to work out Black's reply, which will be on the next line. Points are awarded according to how strong your move is. Try to work out as much as you would in a game — you will gain bonus points for the depth and accuracy of your analysis. Occasionally, I will ask specific questions to test your understanding of the position; the answers appear on the next line and again points are awarded. Keep a note of your scores and compare them with the table below. For the most accurate assessment of your playing strength you should take an average of your scores for all twenty games.

If you are not interested in doing the test, just enjoy the games. My intention was to show off the styles of the leading players in the world, and in that way to give a picture of the current chess scene. Not only that; if these players have made it to the top, this would suggest that they are playing the best and most accurate chess — so their games are the ones from which we can learn the most.

61-70   Grandmaster
51-60   International Master
41-50   FIDE or National Master
31-40   County player
21-30   Club player
11-20   Occasional player
 0-10   Garry Kasparov isn't losing too much sleep over you!

1
A Real Chessplayer

It is a general trend in most sports that the leading players are becoming ever younger. In chess this is certainly the case. A recent arrival into the world top ten is the seventeen-year-old Russian, Vladimir Kramnik.

In 1992, there was great surprise when, on Kasparov's personal insistence, he was chosen as a member of the Russian team to play in the Olympiad — at that time he was virtually unknown outside his own country. His score of 8/9 totally vindicated the selection. Since then Kramnik has firmly established himself amongst the world's leading players with powerful tournament results around the world.

Kasparov has stated on several occasions that he considers Kramnik to be a future challenger for the world title: 'He is definitely the number one talent. I think that he is the only player I have ever seen who does not play worse than I did when I was sixteen … he has a very good natural talent. And you know there is substance. Real chess substance. Many players they're not playing chess, they're playing moves. Kramnik is playing chess.' Praise indeed.

Kramnik's opponent here is International Master Aloisys Kveinys from Lithuania.

Kveinys-Kramnik
Debrecen 1992
Sicilian Defence

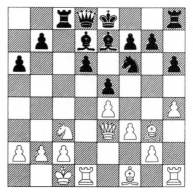

 1 e4 c5 2 ♘f3 d6 3 d4 cxd4 4 ♘xd4 ♘f6 5 ♘c3 ♘c6 6 ♗g5 e6 7 ♕d2 a6 8 0-0-0 h6 9 ♗f4 ♗d7 10 ♗g3 ♖c8 11 f3 ♘xd4 12 ♕xd4 e5 13 ♕e3 ♗e7 14 h4

Start predicting Black's moves now.

14   ...   0-0

Three points. Castling is a sensible move, but it was also possible to play more provocatively with 14 ... b5 (also three points).

White's knight shields the queenside and exerts strong influence over the critical square d5, so dislodging it with ... b5-b4 cannot be bad.

15   ♔b1

15   ...   ♕c7

Two points. Kramnik continues to develop calmly, but I would still be tempted to whip out 15 ... b5 (two points). Deduct one point for 15 ... ♗e6 which loses a pawn to 16 ♗xe5. Careless.

16   ♗d3

16   ...   ♗e6

Three points. This is a beautiful square for the bishop. It is covered from attack by the e5 pawn; protects the d5 square; and points menacingly in the direction of White's king.

Only one point for 16 ... b5, which has lost much of its power now that the king has side-stepped to b1, and c2 is protected by the bishop.

17   ♗h2

17   ...   ♕a5

Six points. It seems curious to move the queen for the second time in the space of a few moves, but Kramnik has spotted a weakness in White's position and seizes upon it

immediately.

18   ♕d2

18   ...   ♖xc3

Three points. The idea behind 17 ... ♕a5 should have been clear: this standard exchange sacrifice was made possible. (I'm sure that if White had seen the possibility of 17 ... ♕a5 he would have chosen 17 ♗e1!, a couple of moves back, covering the knight.)

19   ♕xc3

White has avoided the shattering of his queenside pawns, but Black still has a fierce attack.

19   ...   ♕xa2+

One point.

20   ♔c1

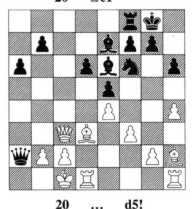

20   ...   d5!

Four points. Unleashing Black's pieces. The queen cuts a lonely figure down on a2, so she desperately needs the rest of her army's support if the attack is going to succeed.

20 ... ♖c8 (one point) looks alright, but it would allow White to exchange queens: 21 ♕a3 ♕xa3 22 bxa3. While it is true that Black does not stand worse - he has a pawn for the exchange, a solid position, and White's queenside pawns are split - a draw would be a likely result; and Kramnik wants more.

21   ♗xe5

21   ...   dxe4

Three points. Two points for 21 ... ♖c8 — a tricky move. If 22 ♕d4 then 22 ... ♗c5 wins immediately; so 22 ♗xf6 should be played. Taking the queen would not leave Black with much of an attack, and 22 ... ♗xf6 allows the queen to be exchanged with 23 ♕a3, so 22 ... gxf6 is the best move, and then the most likely continuation is 23 ♕e1 ♕a1+ 24 ♔d2 ♕xb2 25 ♕g3+ ♔f8. Black still has a strong attack, but in view of his own king's slightly precarious situation, the outcome is not quite clear.

22   ♗xe4

How would you have replied to 22 fxe4 instead?

One point for 22 ... ♖c8, but two for 22 ... ♘g4, with all kinds of nasty threats. If 23 ♗xg7, then 23 ... ♖c8 24 ♕d4 ♗c5 wins; and if 23 ♔d2 (threatening 24 ♖a1) 23 ... ♘xe5 24 ♕xe5 ♗f6. The b-pawn drops and White's king finds itself in no-man's-land between kingside and

queenside.

22   ...   ♘xe4

One point.

23   fxe4

23   ...   ♖c8

Three points. Simple and good: Black's last piece joins the attack.

24   ♕g3

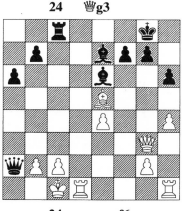

24   ...   f6

One point. Defending against the mate and attacking the bishop, so no time is lost.

25   ♗d4

How would you have responded to 25 ♗c3 here?

25 ... ♕a1+ (two points) 26 ♔d2 ♖d8+ 27 ♔e2 ♗c4+ 28 ♔e3 ♖xd1 wins.

25   ...   ♗b3

Three points. 25 ... ♗b4 (two points) was a tempting alternative. I'm sure that this would be good enough to finish off most players, but White can muster up some kind of defence if he finds 26 c3! ♗b3 27 ♕d3! giving back the exchange, but shutting out Black's queen.

26   ♗c3

26   ...   ♕a1+

One point.

27   ♔d2

27   ...   ♖d8+

One point.

28   ♕d3

28   ...   ♖xd3+

One point.

29   ♔xd3

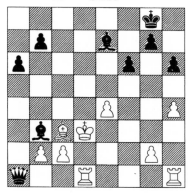

If you foresaw this position when playing 26 ... ♕a1+, then take an extra four points.

29   ...   ♗xc2+

Three points. As his queen and bishop are both attacked, Black must give back a piece, and this is the best way to do it.

30   ♔xc2

The material balance is roughly level (queen and pawn versus two rooks), but Black actually has an excellent position due to White's exposed king and weak pawns. White's real problem is that he has no attack of his own to counter Black's initiative.

30   ...   ♕a4+

One point. A good start. To protect the e-pawn, White must bring his king up the board.

31   ♔d3

31   ...   b5

Four points. An excellent move. White will find it very difficult to meet the dual threats of ... ♕c4+, further harrying the king, and ... b4, dislodging the bishop from its secure post.

32   ♔e3

[Chess diagram]

32   ...   ♗c5+

Two points. The immediate 32 ... b4 would not be so good as after 33

♗d4, the bishop's position is still secure.

33 ♔f4

If White had played 33 ♗d4, how would you have responded?

Two extra points if you found 33 ... ♕b3+ 34 ♖d3 ♗xd4+ 35 ♔xd4 ♕xb2+, winning a second pawn and effectively ending the game.

33 ... ♕c4

Two points. This is the surest way to continue the attack, moving the queen back towards the centre of the board and threatening ... b4, but 33 ... b4 (one point) was also reasonable.

34 ♖d8+

34 ... ♔h7

One point.

35 ♖hd1

35 ... ♕e2

Four points. Highly unpleasant for White. The end of the game is a perfect illustration of the strength of the queen - an all-powerful compact unit - against a diffuse range of weaker pieces attempting to remain protected. The queen is able to zap around the board exploiting the slightest 'looseness' in the enemy position .

36 ♔f5

36 ... b4

Two points. Perfect timing: the bishop must retreat to a miserable square, relinquishing the protection of the b-pawn.

37 ♗e1

37 ... ♕xg2

Two points. Better than taking the b-pawn as it maintains the attack against White's king. The threat is ... ♕h3+ and ... ♗e3 mate. Two bonus points if you played it on the previous turn.

38 e5

38 ... ♕g6+

One point. Not the only way to kill from this position: the same score for 38 ... ♕h3+ or 38 ... ♕f3+.

39 ♔e6

39 ... ♕g4+

One point for this.

40 ♔f7

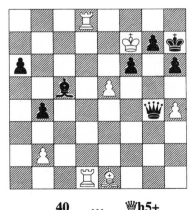

40 ... ♕h5+

One point. Kramnik has found the most efficient way to finish the game. White's king does not escape: 41 ♔e6 ♕xe5+ 42 ♔f7 ♕e7 mate. In view of this, **White resigned**.

There were three phases to this game: the early middlegame, manoeuvring (moves 14 to 17); the attack on the king itself (moves 18-30); and the final kill (moves 31-40). To score well on the first phase, you need some previous knowledge of the Sicilian Defence. Experience would tell you where to position the pieces and which plan to go for; this has little to do with calculation, and even long-term planning, but rather it is the recognition of established patterns and groupings of pieces.

In the second phase you have to look for forcing sequences of moves that bring an advantage, be it material or positional. This involves calculating (if X, then Y, etc.); but also being able to assess the resulting position accurately.

Having liquidated into a position where he correctly assessed that he had a winning advantage, Kramnik finished the game off with great efficiency. The secret of good technique is simple: accurate calculation.

2
Precision Play

The fight through to the final of the World Championship has brought out a sense of purpose in Nigel Short which was previously lacking. He concentrated all his efforts on the Candidates matches, preparing with a thoroughness which is perhaps customary in Eastern Europe, but is unknown to most other English chess professionals.

A good example of his change in approach is his play in the opening. Whereas a few years ago his main aim in this phase of the game would have been to avoid a theoretical struggle, he now actively courts one.

In a sense, Nigel has quite an extreme style. What I mean is, he demands a lot from the position - and he usually manages to get away with it because of his belief in the strategy, and of course his great strength. This game is typical. His opponent is Swedish grandmaster Ulf Andersson, one of the most solid players in the world.

Short-Andersson
Wijk aan Zee 1990
Sicilian Defence

1 e4 c5 2 ♘f3 ♘c6 3 d4 cxd4 4 ♘xd4 g6 5 c4 ♘f6 6 ♘c3 d6 7 ♗e2 ♗g7 8 ♗e3 0-0 9 0-0 ♗d7 10 ♘c2 ♕a5 11 f4 ♖ac8

Now try to predict White's moves.　　　12　♖b1

Four points. The pawn structure here is typical of the 'Maroczy bind' (named after the Hungarian, Geza Maroczy, one of the strongest players of the early part of this century). The pawns on e4 and c4 give White a big space advantage, but with such a centre comes a great deal of responsibility: if the structure crumbles, then White's position could look like an empty shell. So this is Black's task: to break out from his cramped position before he gets squashed; if he manages to do so, the rewards will be great. The fight could be billed as 'Containment v. Counter-attack'.

Moving the rook out of the shadow of the bishop on g7 makes a great deal of sense: one doesn't know if it will be significant, but it certainly reduces the chances of an accident occurring later on.

Two points for 13 ♔h1, another careful move, tucking the king safely in the corner. Nothing for 13 ♕d2 which looks, at first glance, to be the most natural move. This would allow 13 ... ♘g4!; the dark-squared bishop must be retained so 14 ♗xg4 ♗xg4. Black has strong pressure on c3 and soon on c4. This is a typical example of how the position can turn in the space of a couple of moves.

12   ...   a6

13   b4

Two points. This was the other idea behind 13 ♖b1 — but I didn't

want to give the game away. The queen ought to return to base as 13 ... ♕c7 14 ♘d5 ♘xd5 15 exd5 ♘b8 is far too passive.

13   ...   ♕d8

14   ♕d3

Two points. White's centre looks formidable, but it is just at this moment that it is at its most vulnerable. The main problem is that the knight on c3, standing in the line of both Black's bishop and rook, is no longer supported by the b-pawn. Thus a move like 14 b5 (deduct two) would quickly lead to disaster: 14 ... axb5 15 cxb5 ♘a5 with tremendous pressure down the c-file.

If I were playing this position as White, I would invest a great deal of time examining Black's counter-attacking possibilities; it might sound extraordinary, but the game has already reached a critical stage. If White can survive the next few moves without a catastrophe occurring, then the future will look bright. The main shots to be aware of are ... ♘g4 (we have seen that one already); and ... b5.

14 ♔h1 (one point) is a careful move — but perhaps a little too careful. Black could strike with 14 ... b5!; if 15 cxb5 axb5 16 ♗xb5 ♘xb4! 17 ♖xb4 ♖xc3 and White's centre has crumbled. Of course, White does not need to be quite so compliant (16 ♗xb5 is a mistake),

but clearly 14 ♔h1 does not help the cause.

14 ... ♗g4

How would you have replied to 14 ... b5 instead? Be careful.

15 c5 looks promising, but Black actually gets good counterplay after 15 ... dxc5 16 ♗xc5 ♗e6, threatening ... ♘d7.

15 cxb5 is correct, and after 15 ... axb5, not 16 ♘xb5 ♘xe4! 17 ♕xe4 ♗f5, but 16 ♘a3! threatening ♘axb5. The only serious move to counter this is 16 ... ♘xb4, but it seems that White can survive the blitz of tactics: 17 ♖xb4 ♖xc3 18 ♕xc3 ♘d5 19 ♕d2 etc.

Take three extra points if you found both 15 cxb5 and 16 ♘a3. This is a critical variation — it was absolutely necessary to have an answer to 14 ... b5.

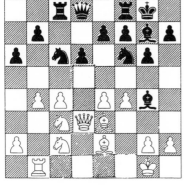

15 ♔h1

Three points. The king is moved to a safer square and the bishop can

now retreat to g1. 15 ♗xg4 would not be good: 15 ... ♘xg4 and the bishop will be exchanged off as 16 ♗d2 is met by 16 ... ♕b6+.

15 ... ♗xe2

16 ♕xe2

One point.

16 ... e6

Black fails to appreciate the seriousness of his situation. At this point, for better or for worse, he should have tried 16 ... b5.

17 c5!

Four points. The point of this move is seen in the variation: 17 ... dxc5 18 ♗xc5 ♖e8 19 ♖bd1 ♕c7 20 e5 ♘d7 21 ♗d6 ♕b6 22 ♘e4. White completely dominates the centre; this was made possible because Black weakened the d6 square with 16 ... e6.

Nothing for other 17th moves — Black was threatening to play ... ♕c7 with pressure on the c-pawn.

17 ... d5

18 ♖fd1

Three points. There is no harm in keeping Black guessing as to how you intend to resolve the central tension. 18 e5 would not be good: Black could break down the centre very quickly with 18 ... ♘d7 and 19 ... f6.

18 ... ♖e8

19 a4

Two points.

19   ...   ♕e7

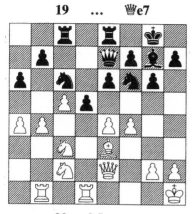

20   b5

One point.

20   ...   axb5

21   e5!

Six points.

21   ...   ♘d7

22   ♘xb5!

Five points. These last two moves were perhaps the most difficult of the whole game. If you recaptured with the a-pawn on either of the last two moves, then I'm afraid no points. The black knight moves to a5, and then to the tremendous square c4; the pawn on c5 could turn out to be very weak.

The other move that is questionable, particularly now that Black has doubled on the e-file, is 21 exd5 earlier — the pin on the bishop makes life too problematic for White.

22   ...   ♖b8

If instead 22 ... ♘xc5, then 23 ♗xc5 ♕xc5 24 ♘d6 wins the exchange.

23   ♘d6

One point.

23   ...   ♖f8

24   ♘d4

Two points. Deduct a point for 24 ♘xb7 ♘dxe5, recovering the pawn.

24   ...   f6

25   ♘xb7

One point. The only way to get anything from the position is to grab a pawn (25 exf6 ♘xf6 is fine for Black).

25   ...   ♘xd4

26   ♗xd4

One point.

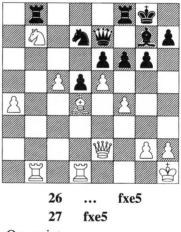

26   ...   fxe5

27   fxe5

One point.

27   ...   ♖f4

How would you have replied to 27

... ♘xe5 instead?

Best is 28 ♗xe5 ♗xe5 (28 ... ♖xb7 29 ♗d6!) 29 ♕xe5 ♖xb7 30 ♖xb7 ♕xb7 31 ♕xe6+. Black is a pawn down and has a miserable defensive task ahead of him. Take two points if you envisaged this sequence.

Andersson prefers to defend more actively.

28　c6

Three points. Forcing Black to give up material, for if 28 ... ♘f8 29 ♗c5, and it all looks a bit grim.

28　...　♖xd4

29　♖xd4

One point.

29　...　♘xe5

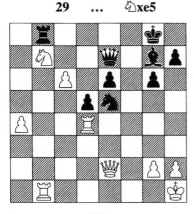

30　♖db4

Three points. White could still end up in difficulties if he is not careful. Short sensibly decides to give up the c-pawn straight away and to break the pin on the knight.

30　...　♘xc6

31　♖b6

One point.

31　...　♘d4

32　♕g4

Two points. A good square. The queen keeps an eye on e6, a sensitive spot in Black's position.

32　...　♖f8

33　a5

Three points. Why not? Black is brewing a counter-attack, but for the moment, he isn't actually threatening anything, so White quietly pushes the a-pawn. Generating a meaningful initiative is going to be difficult with this pawn creeping up the board.

33　...　♗e5

34　a6

One point.

34　...　♕f6

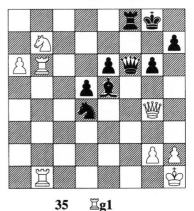

35　♖g1

Two points. By far the best way to defend against the back-rank mate. 35 g3? opens up the king and 35 ♕d1 loses to 35 ... ♕h4!.

35   ...   ♗c7
36   ♖bb1

One point. Keeping the rooks connected is the most sensible.

36   ...   ♕e5

37   ♕h3

Two points. The only alternative was 37 g3, opening up the king — not worthy of serious consideration.

37   ...   ♗b8
38   ♘c5

Four points. The knight's return to the fray decides the issue.

38   ...   ♕d6
39   ♖b7

Two points.

39   ...   h5
40   ♘d7

One point.

40   ...   ♕xa6

And with this, **Black resigned**, as 41 ♖xb8 ♖xb8 42 ♘xb8 ♕b5 43 ♕e3 keeps White a rook up. This was an exceptionally difficult game. Keeping control of the position in the early middlegame takes great vigilance; in a sense it is much easier to play Black than White. The break to be particularly wary of is ... b5 — at every move it should be considered.

In fact, great precision was needed throughout the game; 17 c5! was rather unexpected, and the timing of 21 e5 and 22 ♘xb5 was perfect. Once Short had won the exchange, the position was still very messy, and it required great vigour to convert it to a win.

The lesson to be learned is that it is vital to keep striving for the initiative once you have won material. It is true that Black managed to set up a few threats, but because of the a-pawn's advance, he soon had to fall back on the defensive.

3
Control and Co-ordination

It is often said that Anatoly Karpov has the greatest natural ability of all the top players — including Kasparov. He has an innate sense of where his pieces belong, how they are best co-ordinated, and what is the best pawn structure to build. Because of his talent Karpov has never had to work hard away from the board; he is hardly noted for producing devastating theoretical innovations in the opening.

When he is actually playing is another matter entirely. He is tenacious; a pragmatist; a fighter. There are positions which most other players would have given up as hopeless which he somehow manages to hold or even win. (His game against Seirawan later on in this book is good evidence of that: even though he lost, he did brilliantly just to survive the opening.)

The two words which spring to mind when I think of Karpov's style are control and co-ordination. In this game he is in his element: having got a grip on the position he never let go. His opponent is Grandmaster Johann Hjartarson from Iceland.

Karpov–Hjartarson
Candidates match, Seattle 1989
English Opening

1 c4 e5 2 g3 ♘f6 3 ♗g2 d5 4 cxd5 ♘xd5 5 ♘c3 ♘b6 6 ♘f3 ♘c6 7 0-0 ♗e7 8 a3 ♗e6 9 b4 0-0 10 ♖b1 f6 11 d3 ♕d7

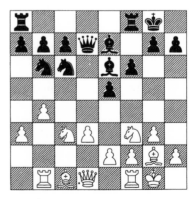

Now start predicting White's moves.

12   ♘e4

Four points. This move contains a threat: 13 ♘c5 ♗xc5 14 bxc5 ♘d5 15 ♖xb7. Two points for 12 ♗b2, 12 ♗e3 and 12 ♗d2, all sound developing moves.

12 b5 (no points) is premature: 12 ... ♘d4 13 ♘xd4?! exd4 14 ♘e4 f5 15 ♘d2 ♗d5, and Black dominates the centre.

12   ...   ♘d5
13   ♕c2

Two points. Beginning the build-up of pressure on the c-file: the usual source of play in Sicilian-type structures.

13 ♗b2 (two points) is strong, preventing Black's knight moving into d4. 13 ♘c5 is impossible: 13 ... ♗xc5 14 bxc5 ♘c3, wins the exchange. Deduct two points if you missed this.

13   ...   b6

Black cuts out the possibility of ♘c5, but leaves the knight on c6 precariously placed.

14   ♗b2

Two points. Preventing the knight moving to d4.

14   ...   ♖ac8
15   ♖bc1

Two points. The same for 15 ♖fc1. One point for 15 b5.

15   ...   ♘d4

If Black had played 15 ... ♘d8,

how would you have replied?

16 d4 (two points) is correct, using the central pawn majority to destroy Black's structure: 16 ... exd4 17 ♘xd4 ♗f7 18 ♖fd1 and White dominates.

16   ♗xd4

One point.

16   ...   exd4
17   ♕c6

Four points. White has an attractive choice here. Two points for 17 ♘xd4, which forces Black to recover the pawn by playing 17 ... ♘xb4; take an extra point if your intended follow-up to this was 18 axb4 ♕xd4 19 b5!, crippling Black's queenside pawns. White is all set to build a strong centre with e3 and d4.

17   ...   ♕xc6
18   ♖xc6

One point. Would you even consider anything else?

18   ...   ♗d7

19 ♘xd4

Six points. An excellent positional sacrifice, which Karpov had clearly envisaged when playing 17 ♕c6.

Nothing for retreating the rook: 19 ♖cc1 c5 20 bxc5 bxc5 when Black could follow up with ... f5 and ... ♘c3 (the big danger for White in this variation).

19 ... ♗xc6

20 ♘xc6

One point. This is just the kind of position which Karpov plays to perfection: he has a bind on his opponent's position; his pieces are well co-ordinated; and he has no weaknesses of his own.

20 ... ♖ce8

21 ♖c1

Two points. Of course, it would be nice to grab a second pawn, but why break co-ordination to do so? It is much better to keep the pressure on Black's position. Besides, if Black did decide to do something about the a-pawn - 21 ... a6 - then White would win material by playing 22 ♘d2, when, curiously, Black's knight has no square to go to.

21 ... f5

22 ♘d2

Two points. It was also possible to play 22 ♘c5 (one point) with the idea 22 ... bxc5 23 ♗xd5+ ♔h8 24 bxc5, when White has two pawns for the exchange and, most importantly, has kept control. But Black may complicate with 22 ... ♘xb4, when Karpov gives 23 ♘d7 ♘xc6 24 ♖xc6 ♗d6 25 ♗d5+ ♔h8 26 ♘xf8 ♖xf8 27 f4 as good for White, but I think that 24 ... ♖f7 gives better chances to defend.

Naturally, Karpov sees no reason to get involved in complications when he has a perfectly adequate alternative.

22 ... ♘f6

23 ♘xa7

One point. The correct moment; Black has no active play at all.

23 ... ♗d6

24 e3

Three points. This is the kind of move which can make a great difference to the game. If 24 ♗f3 g5, threatening ... g4; and if 24 ♔f1 f4, in both cases with irritating counterplay. As well as defending the e-pawn, 24 e3 prevents Black from playing ... f4, the only way in which he may create some open lines for his rooks.

24 ... c5

A good attempt to stir up trouble. White must play very precisely if he is going to hold his advantage.

25 ♘c4

Two points. Keeping Black busy. 25 b5 (two points) is also good, securing a good square for one of the knights on c4. 25 bxc5 (one point) is playable, but only if followed up by 25 ... ♗xc5 26 ♘c4! In fact, I think it is better for Black to play 25 ... bxc5, opening the b-file for his rook.

25 ♘b5 would be a mistake as 25 ... ♖d8 is annoying: White will have to concern himself with the defence of the d-pawn.

25 ... ♗b8

The alternatives were not very jolly: 25 ... ♖d8 26 ♘c6!; or 25 ... ♗c7 26 ♘b5 ♖c8 27 bxc5 bxc5, and now, can you see a simple winning plan for White?

Two extra points for 28 a4, with the idea of pushing it all the way to the eighth rank; there is little that Black can do to prevent it.

26 ♘c6

One point. Preventing Black's rook moving to d8.

26 ... b5

27 ♘4a5

One point. This is not a critical decision; White could also play 27 ♘b6 (one point).

27 ... cxb4

28 axb4

One point.

28 ... ♘d7

This prevents White's threat of ♖c5, snapping up the b-pawn.

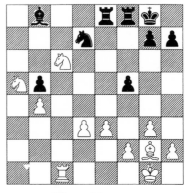

29 d4

Two points. Threatening ♗f1.

29 ... g5!

Black strives to open lines for his rooks.

30 ♘xb8

Three points. It seems a strange decision to exchange off this redundant bishop for the excellently placed knight, so Karpov must be gaining something in return. There were a couple of other ways of meeting Black's threat of 30 ... f4.

Three points for 30 ♗f3, with the idea: 30 ... f4 31 gxf4 gxf4 32 e4, keeping the position closed. Two points for 30 ♔f1, intending: 30 ... f4 31 ♔e2, protecting the pawn-chain, though Black's rooks are now working.

30 ... ♖xb8
31 ♖c7

Three points. The only decent follow-up to taking on b8; have an extra point if you intended this when playing 30 ♘xb8. Putting a rook on the seventh rank is nearly always a good idea, but it becomes a particularly attractive proposition when Black has stripped his king of its pawn cover.

31 ... ♘f6
32 ♘c6

One point.

32 ... ♖b6
33 ♘e7+

One point.

33 ... ♔h8
34 ♘xf5

One point. If you foresaw this position when playing 32 ♘c6, then take an extra two points.

34 ... ♖a6

It is very often the case that when one player wins material, the other gains activity for his pieces. Black's rook threatens to come down to a1 or a2; the f-file is open for the other

rook; and the knight might come to g4. Was it worth a pawn to give Black's pieces so much freedom? You can be certain that it was if Karpov played it, particularly when he had some excellent alternatives at his disposal. He must have foreseen this position when he begun the sequence with 30 ♘xb8, and realised that he would be able to consolidate; but only with some accurate moves.

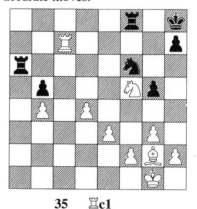

35 ♖c1

Three points. It is necessary to do something about the back-rank. Another way of tackling the problem is 35 h3 (one point), but it isn't quite as good: 35 ... ♖a1+ 36 ♔h2 (36 ♗f1? ♘e4, threatening ... ♘xf2 and ... ♘d2) 36 ... ♖a2, and to make progress White must give up the f-pawn with 37 g4! ♖xf2 38 ♔g3 ♖b2 and Black is still fighting.

35 ... ♖a2
36 h3

One point. To prevent 36 ... ♘g4.

| 36 | ... | ♖b2 |
| 37 | e4 | |

Two points. The b-pawn is irrelevant.

| 37 | ... | ♖xb4 |
| 38 | g4 | |

Two points. Now that the knight is protected, the pawns can steam-roll down the board.

| 38 | ... | h5 |

If 38 ... ♖c4, White should play ...?

39 ♖b1 (two points) is the most accurate, and then back to the plan of pushing the centre pawns. The most important thing is not to exchange the rooks; the passed pawn would give Black serious counterplay. Anyway, when in an ending the exchange down, it is usually best to avoid exchanging off your rook.

| 39 | e5 | |

Two points.

| 39 | ... | hxg4 |

If 39 ... ♘h7 40 e6 wins easily.

| 40 | exf6 | |

One point.

| 40 | ... | gxh3 |
| 41 | ♗xh3 | |

One point.

| 41 | ... | ♖xf6 |
| 42 | ♖c8+ | |

One point.

| 42 | ... | ♔h7 |
| 43 | ♖c7+ | |

Two points. These checks weren't just for fun. The only way now for Black to keep fighting would be to retreat to the back rank — not the best position. White would move the rook behind the b-pawn, then combine pushing the d-pawn with moving his king up the board, depending on how Black reacted.

| 43 | ... | ♔g6 |
| 44 | ♖g7+ | |

One point.

| 44 | ... | ♔h5 |
| 45 | f3 | |

One point. The only way to prevent ♗g4 mate is to give up the rook for the knight, so **Black resigned**.

4
Roll of the Dice

This game is a good old-fashioned king hunt. The vigour of White's play is typical of Larry Christiansen's style: he likes to attack , and will often take considerable risks in striving to gain the initiative — very much the kind of play needed in order to be successful on the American tournament circuit. He is now based in Germany, where he has made a name for himself playing in the national league, and has had considerable success in European tournaments.

Christiansen's opponent in this game is Grandmaster Walter Browne, many times the United States champion, who is also known to be a chancer on the chessboard. The venue for the encounter was perhaps not inappropriate.

Christiansen-Browne
Las Vegas 1990
English Opening

1 c4 e5 2 ♘c3 ♘c6 3 ♘f3 f5 4 d4 e4 5 ♘e5 ♘xe5 6 dxe5 ♘e7 7 ♗g5 h6

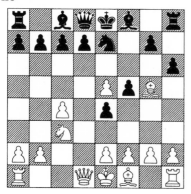

Now try to predict each of White's moves.

8   ♗h4

Four points. Taking would only help Black to develop his pieces; and 8 ♗e3 inhibits White's development; but 8 ♗f4 (two points) was interesting. If 8 ... ♘g6 9 e3 and the queen already threatens to shoot out to h5.

8   ...   c6

If Black had played 8 ... g5 instead, then 9 e3! saves the piece and leaves Black in difficulties: 9 ... ♗g7 10 ♕h5+ ♔f8 11 ♗g3.

9   e3

One point.

9   ...   ♕a5

10   ♗g3

One point. The only sensible way of defending the e-pawn.

10   ...   g6

11   ♗e2

Two points. If you were desperately worried about holding on to the e-pawn and played 11 f4 (one point), I can understand. The problem is that it leaves the position blocked, so it will be harder to make a breakthrough as Black then has enough time to unravel his cramped position.

11   ...   h5

How would you have replied to 11 ... ♗g7?

Two extra points for 12 ♕d6. You can feel the power behind the move. Black's position is completely cut in half.

12   a3

If you found this one, no points, but at least you have the satisfaction

of knowing that your mind works in the same mysterious way as Grandmaster Christiansen. The simplest way to maintain the bind on Black's position is 12 h4 (three points); Black's fixed kingside pawn position looks ugly.

12   ...   h4

13   ♗f4

One point.

13   ...   g5

14   ♗xg5

One point.

14   ...   ♕xe5

Black has managed to rid himself of the crippling e-pawn, but White still has a dangerous lead in development.

15   ♗f4

Two points. A very secure move; the bishop comes back to a more central position with gain of tempo. However, I see nothing wrong with giving a check on h5: 15 ♗h5+ (two points) 15 ... ♔d8, and now White has the choice between the sensible 16 0-0; and the greedy 16 ♗xh4. If Black plays 16 ... f4 then 17 g4! is possible, for if 17 ... fxg3 (e.p.) 18 hxg3! indirectly protects the bishop on h5.

15   ...   ♕f6

16   0-0

Two points. The same for 16 ♗h5+.

16 ... ♘g6

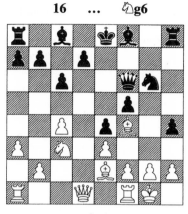

17 ♗c7

If by some brainstorm you came up with this move, take two points, a couple of tranquillisers, and the rest of the week off work. This is one of the daftest moves that I've seen in a long time — and it reflects great credit on Christiansen. Something had to be done about the 'threat' to the bishop on f4. The most sensible, and obvious, move is 17 ♗h5 (two points), which at some point would involve exchanging off this bishop for the knight (the bishop on f4 is the one worth preserving as it is settled on such a good square) but Christiansen must have considered that his advantage would be insufficient in this case.

Not content with a slight advantage, typically, he gambles. 17 ♗c7 promises great rewards if it succeeds, but at the same time entails great risk.

17 ... d6

This is the negative side to 17 ♗c7 — there is a good chance that the bishop will be trapped.

18 f3

Five points. And this is the positive side. While Black is busy trying to ensnare the bishop, White detonates the centre.

18 ... ♕e7

19 ♗a5

Two points. White would not have enough for the piece after 19 fxe4 ♕xc7 20 exf5 ♘e5. This knight would be too strong.

19 ... b6

20 ♕a4

Four points. A very strong move. Only in this way can White obtain sufficient compensation for the piece, so I'm afraid no points for other moves.

20 ... ♕b7

Black must put his queen on a bad square in order to trap the bishop for if 20 ... ♗d7 then 21 ♗xb6; and if 20 ... ♗b7, then ...?

After 21 ♘d5! ♕d8 22 ♗c3 White saves the piece and has a huge attack to boot. An extra point if you found 21 ♘d5.

21 fxe4

Three points. It is time to plunge into the mire since the bishop could no longer be held: 21 ♗b4 a5 is much worse.

21	...	bxa5
22	c5	

Six points. A very important move. For the moment, White's queen is sidelined at the edge of the board. If the attack is to succeed, it is essential that she is brought into the thick of the struggle, and this pawn move clears a path for her into the centre of the board.

One point for 22 exf5.

22	...	♘e5
23	exf5	

Two points. The simplest way of proceeding, but 23 ♕d4 (one point) was also interesting.

23	...	♕g7

Not good. This looks like a move played under time pressure. Instead, how would you have replied to 23 ... dxc5 here?

24 ♕f4 (two points) is the best move (centralisation!). This is better than 24 ♕e4, which takes away an excellent square for the knight. In fact, Black's best chance was to play 23 ... ♗h6, preparing to castle.

24	f6	

Four points. This pawn has the effect of splitting Black's forces.

24	...	♕g6
25	f7+	

Two points. The pawn cannot be captured by the knight because of

♕xc6+, so the king is forced to move — making life very pleasant for the attacker.

This is what it must have been like in the days before the castling rule came in, around the sixteenth century: if you began an attack on the king you could be sure that it wasn't going to slip away to the side of the board in some cowardly manner.

25	...	♔e7
26	♘d5+	

Three points. If the knight is taken then 27 ♕e8 is mate.

26 exd6+ (three points) with the idea 26 ... ♕xd6 27 ♖ad1, was a simple way to continue the attack, and just as good.

26	...	♔d7

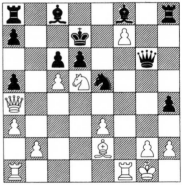

27	♘f6+	

Two points. The same score for 27 ♖ad1.

27 ... ♔e6

The king must walk up the board, for if 27 ... ♔c7 or 28 ... ♔d8 then 29 ♕xa5+ is crunching; and on 27 ... ♔e7 28 cxd6+ is terminal.

28 ♖ad1

Five points. These kind of attacking moves are perhaps the hardest to see. Before embarking upon a forcing sequence of moves, Christiansen calmly brings a rook into the attack: Black's position is such a wreck that there is no chance of him being able to co-ordinate his forces to construct a defence.

Two points for 28 ♘e8, which isn't quite as effective but is more fun.

28 ... ♖b8

From this point, it is possible to calculate right through to the finish.

29 ♗c4+

Two points.

29 ... ♘xc4

30 ♕xc4+

One point.

30 ... ♔e7

How would you have replied to 30 ... d5 instead? (In a game it would have been necessary to have this prepared when playing 29 ♗c4+.)

An extra point for 31 ♖xd5 or 31 ♘xd5, which both win — the former being the most spectacular: 31 ♖xd5 cxd5 32 ♕xd5+♔e7 33 ♕e5+♔xf7 34 ♘d7+ ♔g8 35 ♖xf8+ ♔h7 36 ♖xh8 mate.

31 cxd6+

One point.

31 ... ♔d8

32 ♕xc6

One point.

32 ... ♕xf7

33 ♘d5

One point. The same for 33 ♘e8.

33 ... ♕b7

34 ♕c7+

One point. And here **Black resigned**.

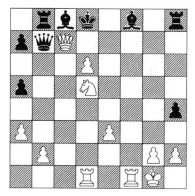

5
Experience v. Youth

Even at the height of his career, Boris Spassky never had a very strong theoretical punch. His strength lay in his attacking ability, his consummate understanding of the middlegame, and excellent technique when finishing off an opponent.

Perhaps I shouldn't be writing in the past tense! Spassky still displays these same characteristics, but his lack of ambition has distorted them: understanding and technique dominate, and he normally prefers to steer the play into calmer waters rather than speculate on an attack.

I am sure Spassky's opponent had this in mind when he plumped for the Benkö Gambit in the game below. No doubt with the latest theory coming out of his ears, he was hoping to engage the former World Champion in a sharp struggle right from the kick-off.

How do you think Spassky will deal with this situation? Will he fight fire with fire? Or will he try to contain the aggression?

Spassky–R. Koch
French Championship 1992
Benkö Gambit

1 d4 ♘f6 2 c4 c5 3 d5 b5 4 cxb5 a6 5 bxa6 g6 6 ♘c3 ♗xa6 7 e4 ♗xf1 8 ♔xf1 d6 9 g3 ♗g7 10 ♔g2 0-0 11 ♘f3 ♘bd7 12 h3 ♕b6 13 ♖e1 ♖fb8

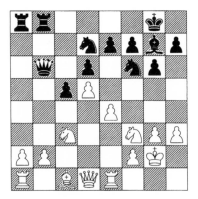

Now start predicting White's moves.

14 ♖e2

Three points. Spassky's choice of variation is already an indication that he wants to play very steadily. Prophylaxis rather than counter-attack is the order of the day. Twenty years ago this system was one of the most popular methods of meeting the Benkö. It lost favour because White players did not enjoy the long defensive task involved, having to be constantly alert to Black's tricks. Even if they managed to emerge from the middlegame unscathed, because of Black's queenside pressure, the ending would more often than not be drawn.

14 ♖e2 is a very sensible move, overprotecting the most sensitive spot in White's position: b2.

14 ♕c2 (three points) is also well motivated.

14 e5 (one point) is premature. After trading on e5, 14 ... dxe5 15 ♘xe5 ♘xe5 16 ♖xe5, 16 ... ♕b7! is a strong move; White is very tied up.

14 ... ♕a6
15 ♕c2

Two points. Another solid move giving more support to c3 and b2. Also two points for 15 ♖c2. For the time being White must tread warily.

A seemingly normal developing move like 15 ♗f4 can lead to disaster: 15 ... ♘h5! 16 ♗g5 (the best move is to go back to square one with 16

♗c1) 16 ... ♖xb2! 17 ♖xb2 ♗xc3 18 ♕c2 ♗xb2 19 ♕xb2 ♘hf6. A typical Benkö position. Black has won the pawn back and retains the initiative because a2 and e4 are so weak. No points for any move with the bishop — but take a point if you spotted the above tactic.

15 ♕e1!? (one point) is an interesting idea, trying to lend weight to the e5 break. It also has the added bonus of overprotecting c3, 15 ... ♘e8 is a good reply though.

15 ... ♘b6
16 a4

Three points. You should have recognised that with 15 ... ♘b6 Black had a concrete positional threat, ... ♘a4, increasing the pressure on the queenside.

16 b3 (one point) is the most obvious way of dealing with this threat, and if White had one more move, then with ♗b2 he could complete his development and have good chances to consolidate the extra pawn. But Black crashes in straight away with 16 ... ♘fxd5!, once again a typical Benkö combination: 17 exd5 (17 ♘xd5 ♗xa1) 17 ... ♗xc3 18 ♕xc3 ♕xe2. At first it looks as though White has good compensation for the exchange after 19 ♗b2 f6 20 ♖e1, but Black is able to liquidate into a favourable ending with 20 ... ♘xd5! 21 ♖xe2 ♘xc3 22 ♗xc3. Although the material balance is roughly even, Black has the better

chances because of his central pawn mass.

Once again, bishop moves are not advisable: 16 ♗f4 ♘a4! or 16 ... ♘c4! leave White struggling to contain Black's initiative.

16 ... ♘fd7

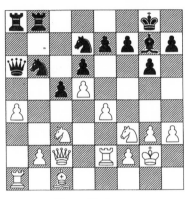

17 ♖a2

Three points. A logical move, removing the rook from the long diagonal — we have already seen that White can easily fall prey to tactics based on the latent power of Black's bishop on g7.

17 ♘b5 (one point) was a very tempting alternative. The complications initiated by 17 ... ♘xd5 are in White's favour: 18 exd5 ♖xb5 19 axb5 ♕xa1 20 ♖xe7; an extra point if you correctly calculated this far. However, if Black calmly defends against the threat of ♘c7 with 17 ... ♖b7, then White has no satisfactory way of parrying ... ♘xa4.

If you were eager to defend your a-pawn with 17 b3 then deduct five! You should be alert to the tactics on the long diagonal by now. Have an extra point if you saw that 17 ... ♗xc3 wins a piece.

17 ♗g5 (no points) at least threatens the e-pawn, but as before, it leaves the queenside too weak; instead of wasting a move defending the pawn, Black seizes the initiative with 17 ... ♘c4! 18 b3 ♘a5 and something is going to drop off.

Back to 17 ♖a2. A question for you: how would you continue if Black decides to grab back his pawn with 17 ... ♗xc3 18 bxc3 ♘xa4? The answer follows after Black's next move ...

17 ... ♘c4

I think this move is a clear mistake. Black's best chance was to capture the pawn as mentioned above. The only way for White to try for the advantage (after 17 ... ♗xc3 18 bxc3 ♘xa4) is to open up the kingside with 19 e5! in the hope that the bishop will be able to infiltrate. Three points if this was your intention. If White hesitates, then Black will keep the position closed with 17 ... f6 and have a free hand on the queenside.

18 b3

Two points. Following Spassky's careful preparation, this move is now possible. There is something very appealing about the move: it connects the heavy pieces.

It wasn't too late to blunder away your position with the tempting 18 ♘b5 (deduct five). A bonus point if you had seen that this fails to 18 ... ♖xb5.

18	...	♘ce5
19	♘xe5	

One point.

19	...	♘xe5
20	♘b5!	

Four points. Right on time. The knight blocks out Black's queen and both rooks; not bad going! If White hesitates for a moment then ... c4 or ... ♘d3 might follow with annoying counterplay. So no points for other moves.

Note that this move is only possible because the rook has moved to a square where it is protected.

20	...	c4

A good attempt to stir up trouble. Be careful!

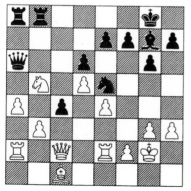

21   ♗f4

Four points. The simplest, intending to trade off Black's most active piece. There were several plausible alternatives, some better than others.

First, 21 ♘c7? (no points) 21 ... ♕a7! 22 ♘xa8 cxb3 23 ♕c7 ♕xa8 24 ♖a1 ♘d3 25 ♖b1 ♖c8 wins material.

21 bxc4?! (only one point) 21 ... ♖c8; after ... ♖xc4 the a-pawn will probably fall as well.

21 b4!? (two points) keeps the position closed, but 21 ... ♖c8! maintaining the c-pawn and preparing ... ♘d3 is irritating. Black's knight is a monster.

21 f4! (four points) is certainly the best of the bunch: 21 ... cxb3 22 ♕xb3 ♘d7 23 ♗e3 leaves White with a dominating position. I'm sure that Spassky preferred the game continuation to this line because here White must always be careful about his king: having played f4 the second rank is potentially weak.

21	...	♖c8
22	♗xe5	

Two points. Normally it would be criminal to exchange off a bishop for a knight like this, but in the preceding moves Spassky has removed everything from the long diagonal (17♖a2, 18 b3, 20♘b5) so Black's bishop just fires into space. It is clear from the variations in the last note that the knight is the source of Black's counterplay, so this move cuts the Gordian knot.

22	...	cxb3
23	♕xb3	

One point.

23	...	♗xe5
24	♖ec2	

Two points. The position is clearly technically winning for White, but that does not mean that it is easy to win it. Were you tempted by 24 f4 (no points) 24 ... ♗g7 25 e5? White's centre certainly looks impressive, but this would be a good way to jeopardise the win: White's king is exposed and 25 ... ♖c5! is a reminder that the d-pawn is weak.

24	...	♖xc2
25	♕xc2	

One point.

25	...	♖c8
26	♕e2	

Two points. Also two for 26 ♕b3. How would you continue if Black now played 26 ... ♖c5, halting the advance of the a-pawn?

26	...	♕a5

If instead 26 ... ♖c5, then two bonus points if you found the excellent move 27 ♘d4!. Exchanging queens further simplifies the position, and with the rook behind the passed pawn the ending is an easy win; moving the

queen allows ♘c6! facilitating the advance of the a-pawn.

27	♖c2

Two points. Simple and effective. With every exchange White is a step nearer his goal. Now Black's queen is tied down to stopping the a-pawn.

27	...	♖xc2
28	♕xc2	

One point.

28	...	♕e1

29	♘a7!

Five points. Great move.

White must find a way to get the a-pawn rolling. 29 ♘a3 (only one point) with the idea of ♘c4 is the other way of going about it, but this allows the bishop to assume an excellent diagonal: 29 ... ♗d4! ties White's queen down to the defence of f2, and the win is already in doubt. If 30 ♘c4 ♗xf2!.

29	...	♗c3

30 ♘c6

Two points. It should have been fairly obvious where this one was heading.

This is a wonderful square. The knight forces both queen and bishop to keep an eye on the a-pawn: it prevents the bishop from moving to d4; and it hits a sensitive point near to Black's king.

30 ... ♔f8

31 ♕d3

Two points. Threatening ♕e3 forcing an exchange of queens. Black has to contort himself to prevent it.

31 ... ♗d2

32 ♕d4

Three points. All Spassky needs to do is get his queen in near Black's king and the game will be over. This move forces a slight weakness in Black's position.

32 ... f6

33 h4

Two points. Deduct a couple if you lunged in with your queen: 33 ♕a7? ♕xe4+ defends the threatened pawn on e7.

33 ... h5

34 ♕d3

Three points. The start of the decisive manoeuvre. Take two if you wanted to play this on the last move.

34 ... ♔f7

Black can only wait. If the bishop or queen move the a-pawn advances.

35 ♕f3!

Two points.

35 ... ♕a1

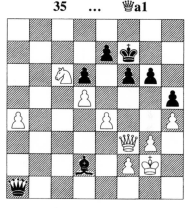

36 g4!

Three points. If you saw this idea a couple of moves ago when manoeuvring your queen, take two bonus points.

36 ... ♕xa4

37 gxh5

One point.

37 ... gxh5

38 ♕xh5+

One point.

38 ... ♔g7

39 ♕g4+

One point. Will anyone admit to playing 39 ♘xe7? Off with your head!

39 ... ♔f8

40 ♕e6!

Two points. The knight even prevents the queen from returning to defend the pawn. **Black resigned**.

Superb technique from Spassky. His opponent didn't have a hint of counterplay.

6
Genesis of a Champion

Although Gary Kasparov had managed to fight his way to the top of the chess world by bamboozling many of his opponents with dynamic sacrifices, he found that this style was inadequate against the coolness and precision of Anatoly Karpov. In order to scale the final peak he was forced to control his aggression, and in so doing became a more rounded player. The game I've selected is from Kasparov's early days (he was just fourteen at the time) when pawns didn't count for so much. His opponent is a local rival from Baku, Eldar Magerramov, who has since become a Grandmaster. This was actually a training game, and it is safe to assume that a great deal of it was prepared in advance by Kasparov: his wildest games are often the result of thorough homework.

Magerramov-Kasparov
Baku 1977
Queen's Gambit Declined
1 ♘f3 ♘f6 2 d4 e6 3 c4 d5 4 ♘c3 ♗e7 5 ♗g5 h6 6 ♗h4 0-0 7 e3 b6 8 ♕b3 ♗b7 9 ♗xf6 ♗xf6 10 cxd5 exd5 11 ♖d1

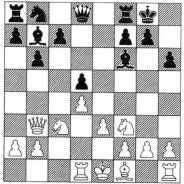

Start predicting Black's moves now.

11 ... c5

Four points. An explosive move, typical of Kasparov's style in his youth. A few years later, arriving at the same position, he was able to curb his natural instincts and played the more conservative (and correct) 11 ... ♖e8; in contrast to this game, the players embarked on some painstaking manoeuvring: 12 a3 c6 13 ♗d3 ♘d7 14 0-0 ♘f8 15 ♗b1 g6 16 ♖fe1 ♘e6 17 ♗a2 ♕c7 (Korchnoi-Kasparov, Candidates match, London 1983). Black is still aiming to break the position open with c5, liberating the bishops, but he prepares for it carefully first.

Four points for 11 ... ♖e8; and two points for 11 ... c6 preparing ... ♘d7.

12   dxc5

12   ...   ♘d7

Four points. The only correct follow-up. If instead 12 ... bxc5 13 ♕xb7; and taking on c3 doesn't help much either.

13   c6

Accepting the pawn sacrifice with 13 cxb6 was the critical continuation. How would you have then proceeded?

13 ... ♘c5 (two points) is best, gaining a tempo on the queen before capturing on b6. Whether Black has enough for the pawn is difficult to say: this was definitely the way to test the correctness of the pawn sacrifice.

13   ...   ♗xc6

One point. Nothing for the intermediate move 13 ... ♘c5, which might have a point if White played 14 ♕xd5 ♗xc3+ 15 bxc3 ♕xd5 16 ♖xd5 ♗xc6, when Black has some compensation for the pawn, but fails to 14 cxb7 ♘xb3 15 bxa8(♕) ♕xa8 16 axb3. Two minor pieces and a rook is too high a price to pay for the queen.

14   ♘d4

What should you play in reply to 14 ♘xd5 here?

14 ... ♘c5 (two points) is once

again the move. White should play 15 ♕c4 keeping the knight protected, then 15 ... ♗xb2; Black's position holds together because of his well-posted knight on c5 (no pawns can attack it). Luckily, White does not have any useful discovered attack with his knight.

14   ...   ♗xd4

Three points. From a strategic point of view, it looks curious to give up the bishop, but the move should be seen as the start of a powerful forcing sequence. (If 14 ... ♗b7, White can simply capture the pawn on d5.)

15   ♖xd4

From this point, try and work out what Kasparov's attacking idea is. If White had played 15 exd4, what would be your reply?

15 ... ♕g5 (two points) is irritating for White. He must first play 16 g3 before developing the bishop, then 16 ... ♕f5 looks like a good move: if 17 ♗e2 ♕h3; and if 17 ♗g2 ♖fe8+. White has difficulty castling.

Note that 15 ... ♖e8+ would not be so effective: 16 ♗e2, and White castles on the next move.

15   ...   ♘c5

Four points. Essential. If Black routinely plays ... ♖e8, or ... ♘f6, then White will play 16 ♗e2 and 17 0-0 with the better position: it wouldn't take much effort to gang up on the isolated d-pawn with ♗f3 and ♖fd1. The position plays itself.

16 ♕d1

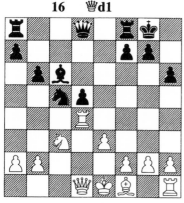

16 ... ♘e6

Two points.

17 ♖d2

17 ... d4

Five points. This is the point of the sequence begun by 14 ... ♗xd4. Kasparov sacrifices a pawn to open the long diagonal and the e-file. If you realised after 15 ♖xd4 that this was the big idea, then take another four points.

18 exd4

18 ... ♖e8

Three points. The best way to proceed. If 18 ... ♘f4, then White may defend by playing 19 f3 — the king crawls out to f2 if the rook checks.

19 f3

If White had played 19 d5, how would you have replied? (You will need to think more than one move ahead.)

The correct sequence is 19 ... ♘f4+ 20 ♗e2 ♘xg2+ 21 ♔f1 ♗d7!. Three extra points if you got this far. White's king is in desperate trouble; the knight cannot be captured because of 22 ♔xg2 ♕g5+ 23 ♔f1 ♗h3+ 24 ♔e1 ♕g2.

19 ... ♗xf3

Six points. It is rather extraordinary that Black does not have a lethal discovered check at his disposal. 19 ... ♘f4+ (three points) is the best of them: 20 ♔f2 ♕e7! 21 ♗a6 ♕e3+ 22 ♔f1, and White's position is unenviable.

Nothing for 19 ... ♘xd4+ which leads to a draw: 20 ♔f2 ♕e7! 21 ♖xd4 ♕e3+ 22 ♔g3 ♕e5+ 23 ♔f2 etc.

20 gxf3

20 ♕xf3 ♘g5+ wins the queen.

20 ... ♕h4+

Two points.

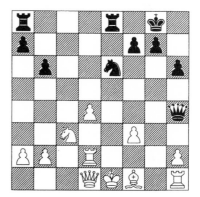

21	♖f2
21	...	♘xd4+

Two points.

22	♗e2
22	...	♘xf3+

One point. Kasparov has completely destroyed White's defences.

23	♔f1
23	...	♕h3+

One point.

24	♖g2
24	...	♘h4

One point.

| 25 | ♖g1 |

It should have been reasonably easy to calculate up to this point (two extra points if you foresaw this position when playing 20 ... ♕h4+) as White's moves were all forced. Now you must decide how to move in for the kill.

| 25 | ... | ♖ad8 |

Four points. Kasparov brings another rook into the attack, clearly the best continuation. It would be a mistake to play 25...♘xg2: there is really no need to cash in yet, keeping White tied up is a much more effective plan.

26	♕e1
26	...	♖d3

Two points. Preventing White's 'threat' of 27 ♕g3 forcing an exchange of queens.

| 27 | ♕f2 |

In this remarkable position White is bound hand and foot.

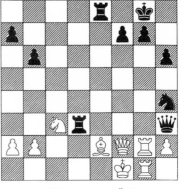

| 27 | ... | ♘f3 |

Four points. A neat way to finish the game. White has no sensible move left: the rook on g2 is pinned to the king; the king has no legal move; 28.♗xf3 ♖xf3 loses the queen; 28.♗xd3 ♘xh2 mate; and if 28 ♕g3, Black plays ...?

28 ... ♘d2+ (one point) 29 ♔e1 ♖xg3 30 ♖xg3 ♘f3+! 31 ♔f2 ♘xg1 with a decisive material advantage.

28	♖h1
28	...	♖de3

Three points. 29 ♗xd3 was threatened.

29	♖g1
29	...	♔h8

One point. A careful move, though not strictly necessary as ♖xg7+

wasn't actually threatened.

30   ♖h1

30   ...   b5

Four points. This could have been played on the last move instead of 29 ... ♔h8; balance up your score if you did so. Here **White resigned** as it is impossible to prevent 31 ... b4 dislodging the knight (31 a3 a5), after which 32 ... ♖xe2 wins.

To score well on this game you needed to have two particular strengths: good tactical imagination; and the ability to calculate accurately.

The former, one gains mainly through experience — familiar landmarks appear which can trigger off ideas. In this game, for instance, I would see that my opponent had delayed castling, and then would look for some way in which I could trap his king in the centre.

On the other hand, the latter can be practised and improved simply by knowing the processes involved. In open positions, such as the one which arose in this game, it is necessary to calculate a great deal.

(What I mean by calculation is: 'if I play X, then he must play Y, then I have a choice of Q or Z' and so on.) The secret of good calculation lies not in the depth of analysis, but rather its relevance, i.e. in knowing what to analyse, and how far to go down a particular line. That involves two things: first, in a given position, selecting likely first moves (in Think like a Grandmaster [Batsford, 1971] Kotov describes these as 'candidate' moves); and second, being able to assess positions accurately. For instance, after 19 f3, Kasparov would have first seen that 19 ... ♘f4+ 20 ♔f2 ♕e7 21 ♗a6 ♕e3+ 22 ♔f1 offered him good attacking chances; then he might have gone back to the starting position and realised that 19 ... ♗xf3 was even better than this first variation. I cannot imagine that his initial calculations would have gone very much beyond 24 ... ♘h4; it would have been enough to have seen this position and realised that, one way or another, Black had a winning advantage — if only on material (rook and two connected pawns should be winning against two minor pieces).

7
A King in Exile

'Solitude gives birth to the original in us, to beauty unfamiliar and perilous — to poetry. But also it gives birth to the opposite: to the perverse, the illicit, the absurd.'

Thomas Mann

After the farce of his comeback match in Belgrade last Autumn, I never imagined that I would ever feel any sympathy for Bobby Fischer.

There is the question of the morality of playing in a match organised by Serbia, the main instigators of an horrific civil war; and sponsored by a man with a less than wholesome reputation. It is alleged that Jezdimir Vasiljevic, the boss of the JugoSkandic banking corporation which put up the phenomenal prize fund, made his pile through illegal arms trading. To add to the bad aroma of the whole event, Fischer used the occasion to express some of his own vile political ideas, including his anti-semitic views.

There was something else too. Hans Ree, writing in the superb Dutch journal *New In Chess*, hit the nail on the head when he said: '…to me there is something creepy about this match. A repetition of Reykjavik 1972. It's scheduled to start exactly twenty years to the day that Spassky resigned in the last game there.'

Even the officials who were at the match in 1972 had been re-invited — at least those who were still alive. 'Just like the old days, when everything in the garden was lovely.'

But the latest chapter in the saga has actually left me feeling some sympathy for Fischer, who appears more naive and unworldly than anything else. The JugoSkandic bank collapsed at the beginning of February 1993, at which point Vasiljevic made a swift exit to Israel. He is reported to have arrived there with a suitcase bulging full of money — and Fischer's passport in his pocket. Fischer was supposedly only paid half his money, and remains in the Belgrade Intercontinental vainly waiting for Vasiljevic to settle his bill.

Where Fischer goes from here is unclear. He certainly is not welcome back in the USA, where he actually faces imprisonment for 'dealing with the enemy': an obscure law dating back to the time of the First World War, but which in media jargon might be described as 'sanctions-busting'. And whether there is another organiser prepared to put up with Fischer's bizarre demands - or indeed find for him an opponent as accommodating as Spassky - is doubtful.

This game is from the time when Fischer was at the height of his powers. His opponent is Ulf Andersson from Sweden who, at the time of this game was just beginning his career, but later became one of the strongest grandmasters in the world.

Fischer-Andersson
Exhibition game, Siegen 1970
Nimzowitsch-Larsen Attack

1 b3 e5 2 ♗b2 ♘c6 3 c4 ♘f6 4 e3 ♗e7 5 a3 0-0 6 ♕c2 ♖e8 7 d3 ♗f8 8 ♘f3 a5 9 ♗e2 d5 10 cxd5 ♘xd5 11 ♘bd2 f6 12 0-0 ♗e6

Try to predict each of Fischer's moves from here.

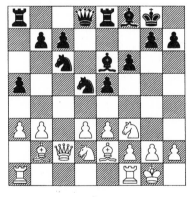

13 ♔h1

Four points. Inspired. If any of you found this move then it is a

minor miracle. A normal human being might play 13 ♖ac1 here (three points); or perhaps 13 ♘e4 (three points) preparing to put the knight in to c5. Even 13 d4 (two points) was possible, though dissipating the central tension at such an early stage would not be to Fischer's taste: 13 ... exd4 14 ♘xd4 ♘xd4 15 ♗xd4 is a bit dull.

Fischer dabbled with 1 b3 on a few occasions in 1970, notching up some notable scalps: Mecking and Tukmakov amongst them. Mostly the games transposed, like this one, into a Sicilian reversed — which naturally RJF was quite at home in. The formation he has employed is what we nowadays call a 'hedgehog' (see game 10, Vukic-Suba, for a full discussion of the ideas behind the system). Although commonplace now, the system was relatively new in 1970; Fischer was one of those who did much to popularise it by demonstrating, in games like this, that it also has great attacking potential.

13	...	**♛d7**
14	**♖g1**	

Three points. 13 ♔h1 had to be good for something. However, if you are of strong character and simply didn't like the whole plan, then I'll give you two points for 14 ♔g1!, retracing Fischer's step. White's position is strong enough to withstand some to-ing and fro-ing.

14	...	**♖ad8**
15	**♘e4**	

Two points. This is a key square in this opening. As mentioned above, the knight might be angling for c5, or it might have designs on the kingside. Black is unable to lash out with 15 ... f5: 16 ♘eg5 or 16 ♘c5 picks off one of the bishops.

One point for something normal like 15 ♖ac1.

15	...	**♛f7**

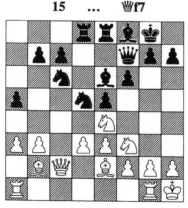

16   g4!

Four points. If you realised that

this was going to be the big idea earlier on, then have another point. It looks outrageous to move a pawn up virtually in front of the king; but here White can get away with it because he has enough pieces around his king, and an excellent central structure (f2, e3, d3) preventing any irritating threats. As well as being the prelude to a kingside attack, moving the pawn to g4 makes sound positional sense: it secures the outpost for the knight on e4.

Of course, moving the queen from d7 permitted the thrust. If Black had 'passed' for a move, then White would have had to prepare g4 with h3. If on the previous move you wanted to play 15 h3 intending g4, instead of 15 ♘e4, then take two points.

16	...	**g6**

If Black hadn't played this, then White would have been able to open a file straight away on the kingside, e.g. 16 ... ♔h8?! 17 g5! f5 18 g6! hxg6 19 ♘eg5 ♛f6 20 ♘xe6 ♛xe6 21 ♘g5 ♛f6 22 ♛c4! with a lethal attack. Take an extra two points if you spotted this idea.

17	**♖g3**	

Two points.

17	...	**♗g7**
18	**♖ag1**	

Two points. Once g4 has been played, it is clear where the future lies for White, so nothing for alternatives to the last two moves. Although for the moment it is impossible to open the g-file, the day is bound to come.

18 ... ♘b6
19 ♘c5

One point. The most natural way to protect the b-pawn.

19 ... ♗c8
20 ♘h4

Three points. A strong manoeuvre. White must be patient in order to gain further ground on the kingside. 20 g5, attempting to open a file, would be solidly met by 20 ... f5; while advancing the h-pawn does not achieve much — when it gets to h5, Black just closes the position with ... g5.

20 ... ♘d7
21 ♘e4!

Two points. Exchanging off pieces only eases Black's cramped position.

21 ... ♘f8

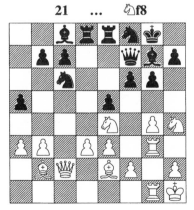

22 ♘f5!

Caramba. Four points. Disaster occurs on the g-file if Black accepts the piece. Taking with the bishop is also miserable: 22 ... ♗xf5 23 gxf5 g5 24 ♘xg5! isn't bad (among others).

22 ... ♗e6
23 ♘c5

One point. Once again, the best way to defend the b-pawn, counter-attacking at the same time.

23 ... ♘e7
24 ♘xg7

Two points and nothing for other moves. Removing this piece is strategically very important: The shadow of White's bishop on b2 now casts itself over Black's kingside — it has no opponent.

24 ... ♔xg7
25 g5!

Four points. Opening the long diagonal for the bishop, as well as the g-file for the rooks. This is the decisive break.

25 ... ♘f5
26 ♖f3

Two points. The most irritating move. 26 gxf6+ is also good (but worth only one point). There is no point in resolving the tension if it is not necessary. After 26 ♖f3, Black gets ripped apart if he captures on g5: 26 ... fxg5 27 ♗xe5+ ♔g8 and now 28 ♘e4 or 28 e4 are both good.

26   ...   b6
27   gxf6+

Two points. Typically, Fischer selects the clearest way of prosecuting his attack. Only one point for 27 ♘e4.

27   ...   ♔h8
28   ♘xe6

One point.

28   ...   ♖xe6
29   d4!

Two points. Take an extra two points if, as Fischer had obviously done, you had envisaged this position when playing 27 gxf6 +.

29   ...   exd4
30   ♗c4

One point. The bishops are lethal.

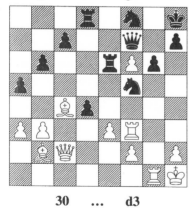

30   ...   d3

Black is bust whatever he does, but this move leaves White with no difficult decisions to make at all. 30 ... c5 would at least try to cut out

one of the bishops, and sets up a potential trick on the long diagonal with ... ♕b7. What would you play now?

The clearest continuation is 31 ♖xf5! (much stronger than capturing the exchange which allows Black to set up some sort of defence) 31 ... gxf5 32 ♕xf5. The immediate threat is ♖g7. Black cannot capture on f6 because of the mate on g8; and 32 ... ♕b7+ is met simply by 33 f3. Two points if you saw this decisive sacrifice.

31   ♗xd3

One point. Again, the simplest.

31   ...   ♖xd3
32   ♕xd3

One point.

32   ...   ♖d6
33   ♕c4

One point. One point for 33 ♕e4 as well.

33   ...   ♘e6
34   ♗e5

One point. Unlucky. Score six points, and prepare for a shower of gold coins on your chessboard, if you noticed 34 ♖xf5!! gxf5 35 ♖g7 ♕f8 36 ♕xe6!! ♖xe6 37 f7 ♕xg7 38 f8 (♕). I suppose, because the position is so easily winning, Fischer had relaxed a little.

34   ...   ♖d8
35   h4

One point. Continuing the kingside assault in fairly mechanical fashion. 35 ♖xf5 (three points) still isn't bad: 35 ... gxf5 36 ♖g7 ♕h5, threatening ... ♕f3+, fails to the calm 37 ♔g2! and there is no defence to the mating attack.

| 35 | ... | ♘d6 |
| 36 | ♕g4 | |

One point. The queen belongs on the kingside. A point for 36 ♗xd6 too.

| 36 | ... | ♘f8 |
| 37 | h5 | |

One point. Consistent. The kingside is slowly, but surely, prised open.

| 37 | ... | ♘e8 |
| 38 | e4 | |

One point. In Fischer's games one usually doesn't have to wait thirty-eight moves before this is played. Closing the long diagonal towards the king is sensible.

| 38 | ... | ♖d2 |
| 39 | ♖h3 | |

Two points. Having played e4, this is now possible.

| 39 | ... | ♔g8 |
| 40 | hxg6 | |

One point.

| 40 | ... | ♘xg6 |
| 41 | f4 | |

One point. The most forceful, threatening f5.

| 41 | ... | ♔f8 |
| 42 | ♕g5 | |

One point. Threatening ♕h6+ and f5.

| 42 | ... | ♘d6 |
| 43 | ♗xd6+ | |

One point. And here, Andersson decided that he had had enough. **Black resigned.** After such a striking and well-executed middlegame, it is a pity that the finish was, by the highest standards, a little lacklustre.

I don't know whether Fischer's plan of ♔h1, ♖g1 and g4 was his own invention; he had actually already played it in a game four years previously — with Black:

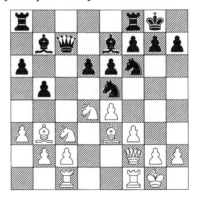

Soruco - Fischer
Havana Olympiad 1966.

14 ... ♔h8 15 ♘ce2 ♖g8 16 ♔h1 g5 17 h3 ♖g6 18 ♘g3 ♖ag8.

This position might be even better than in the game against Andersson:

it is much easier to open lines on the kingside with h5 and g4 now that White has played h3. The game actually came to an abrupt conclusion before the attack was set in train: 19 ♘xe6? fxe6 20 ♗xe6 ♘xe4 21 ♘xe4 ♖xe6 0-1.

Whether the plan was original or not is really a moot point. Fischer was certainly one of the first to understand the importance of the idea and to employ it in top-level chess.

8
A Question of Technique

When two fairly evenly matched players meet each other, it will usually be necessary for one of them to unbalance the position in order to attempt to win. Just occasionally however, one might be lucky enough to gain an advantage early on in the game which, with accurate play, will be sufficient to force victory: the game becomes a dreaded 'matter of technique'. It might be the win of a pawn; possession of an open file; or domination of a diagonal.

In this game, Jonathan Speelman finds himself with the superior pawn structure and the two bishops right in the opening. As the position is relatively simple, it ought to be possible for him to win without resorting to great complications. The game was played at the annual Lloyds Bank open in 1992, which Speelman went on to win. His opponent is Ilya Gurevich from the USA - who, I should add, normally plays much better than this.

I. Gurevich-Speelman
London (Lloyds Bank) 1992
Caro-Kann Defence
1 e4 c6 2 c4 d5 3 exd5 cxd5 4 cxd5 ♘f6 5 ♗b5+ ♘bd7 6 ♘c3 a6 7 ♕a4 ♖b8 8 ♗xd7+ ♕xd7 9 ♕b3

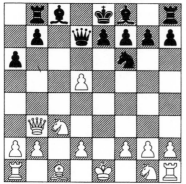

Start predicting Black's moves now.

9 ... b5

Four points. It is best to try to recover the pawn immediately. 9 ... g6 (one point) was also possible, preparing to develop the kingside, but it might turn out to be a little slow: 10 d4 ♗g7 11 ♗f4! and White is gaining valuable time.

10 ♘ge2
10 ... ♗b7

Three points. The simplest: the bishop, which was blocked in by the queen, moves to its strongest position — on the long diagonal, and Black is ready to capture on d5.

10 ... b4 (no points) also looks good, but for the moment there is no real threat to the knight because of ♕xb8.

11   ♘f4
11   ...   g5

Six points. It looks bizarre to throw the pawn up the board away from its comrades, but because White is so under-developed it is impossible to exploit.

Recapturing the pawn by 11 ... ♖d8 looks heavy-handed: it will involve giving up the bishop pair, and as we shall see, this can be a game-winning asset.

12   ♘ge2
12   ...   ♘xd5

One point. If you ignored my comments on the previous move and captured with the bishop - 12 ... ♗xd5 - then deduct two. Black would still retain some advantage after this, but it would be considerably less than in the game.

13   ♘xd5

Tricky.

13   ...   ♕xd5

Two points. Speelman would be quite happy to go into an ending: his radiating bishops and superior pawn structure (White's d-pawn is isolated) give him a technically winning position. White was hoping for 13 ... ♗xd5? 14 ♕g3 attacking both the pawn on g5 and the rook on b8.

14   ♕g3

Avoiding the ending, but leaving Black's queen and bishop as a powerful battery directed exactly where White's king is about to castle.

14   ...   ♖d8

Two points. Preferable to 14 ... ♖c8 (one point): it feels right to bear down on the isolated d-pawn.

15   0-0

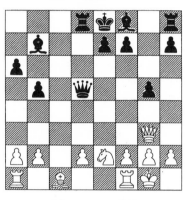

15   ...   h5

Six points. This looks outlandish, but it keeps White on the defensive and ensures that Black maintains control. The threat is ... h5-h4-h3, smashing open the h-file as well as the long diagonal.

At first glance the most natural move in the position is 15 ... ♗g7, developing the bishop on the long diagonal and preparing to castle. It would certainly be good if the pawn were on g6 rather than g5, but here White could play 16 d4! h6 (to protect the g -pawn) 17 ♗e3 0-0 18 f4!, and Black's king is suddenly coming under fire. Nevertheless, two points for 15 ... ♗g7 (it is not necessary for Black to be as co-operative as in the last variation).

16   h3

16   ...   h4

One point.

17   ♕g4

The queen must keep defending g2.

17   ...   b4

Three points. Constricting White further — and very much in Speelman's style. This pawn move ensures that Black's queen will never be attacked by ♘c3, and therefore the mate threat is maintained.

17 ... f5 does not win: 18 ♕xg5 ♖g8 19 ♕h5+ ♔d7 20 f3 puts a stop to the immediate threats.

18   d4

18   ...   f6

One point. A solid move, keeping everything protected, but 18 ... e6 (three points) might well gain a move over the game. White cannot take on g5 with either queen or bishop: 19 ♕xg5? ♕xg5 20 ♗xg5 ♖g8! 21 ♗xd8♖xg2+22♔h1♖xf2+23♔g1 ♖g2+24♔h1♖xe2+etc. I think you get the picture; or 19 ♗xg5 ♖g8 20 f4 f6 winning a piece.

19   f3

19   ...   e6

Two points. It is time to get the bishop out.

20   ♗d2

20   ...   ♗e7

Two points. With the lethal threat of 20 ... f5 winning the queen. White's reply is forced.

21   f4

21   ...   f5

One point. Definitely no points for 21 ... gxf4 22 ♘xf4! ♕xd4+ 23 ♔h1 when White's attack is more dangerous than Black's, e.g. 23 ... ♕xd2 24 ♕g6+ ♔d7 25 ♖ad1 wins.

22   ♕f3

22   ...   g4!

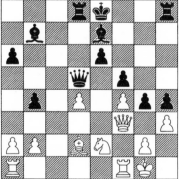

Four points. Stronger than 22 ... ♕xf3 23 gxf3 gxf4 24 ♗xf4 which allows White's minor pieces some mobility. In bypassing the pawn on f4 Black ensures that the knight and bishop remain permanently blocked in.

23   ♕xd5
23   ...   ♗xd5

One point. If you recaptured with
the pawn, blocking in the pride of
Black's position, the bishop on b7,
then I despair (I leave it at your own
discretion as to how many points to
deduct).

24   ♖fc1

If White had captured on g4 (24
hxg4) instead, how would you have
continued?

A leading question if ever there
was one. The simple 24 ... fxg4
gives White some freedom after 25
f5! allowing the knight and bishop
into play via f4.

24 ... h3! (three points) is much
stronger: it is true that after 25 gxh3
♖xh3 26 g5 there is no immediate
win, but once the other rook comes
into play White's king will be cut to
shreds. Therefore Black plays 26 ...
♔d7! and ... ♖h8!. Note once again
that by leaving the white pawn on
f4, the bishop and knight are unable
to find reasonable squares.

24   ...   gxh3

One point.

25   gxh3
25   ...   ♖g8+

Three points.

26   ♔f2

26   ...   ♖g2+

Two points. There are certain pairs
of pieces which complement each
other very well: queen and knight
can be a lethal attacking force; king
and knight combine well in defence;
and in the endgame, as the last couple
of moves have demonstrated, rook
and bishop are a powerful team.

I have played endgames of rook
and bishop versus rook and knight
where, despite being a couple of
pawns down, I have managed to
draw or occasionally even win. Of
course it depends on many factors -
whether the bishop is adequately
supported, king position, passed
pawns, etc. - but it is still something
to bear in mind.

Take an extra couple of points if
you foresaw the rook's entry into
White's position when you captured
on h3.

27   ♔e3
27   ...   ♖h2

Two points. Tying White down
further.

28   ♘g1
28   ...   ♔d7

Three points. Very simple.
White's rook is not permitted to
enter the position ...

29   ♗e1
29   ...   ♖g8

... and the other rook is brought
into play. One point.

30   ♗f2
30   ...   ♖gg2

Two points.

31   ♖c2

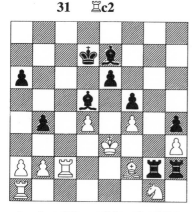

A miserable position for White: he is bound hand and foot; yet Black still needs to break through. How?

31   ...   e5

Six points. A beautiful move, enabling the dark-squared bishop to enter the game with decisive effect. If 32 dxe5 ♖xf2! 33 ♖xf2 ♗c5+ wins; or 32 fxe5 ♗g5+ and ... ♖xf2.

There was another way to break through: 31 ... ♗d6 (three points) threatening to win a pawn with 32 ... ♗xf4+, is more prosaic but no less effective. If 32 ♖f1 then 32 ... ♗xa2 snaffles a pawn.

32   ♖f1
32   ...   exf4+

Two points. Once the position opens White cannot avoid losing material.

33   ♔xf4
33   ...   ♗e4

One point.

34   ♖e2
34   ...   ♗g5+

Two points for this as well as the immediate 34 ... ♗d3. Here **White resigned** as after 35 ♔e5 ♗d3 Black will win at least a rook. An excellent technical display from Speelman: Gurevich was not given a shred of counterplay.

9
Luddite

'Imagine you are sitting beside the latest mainframe multi-processor computer, capable of analysing to a depth of 60 ply, try and guess its moves...'

Is it possible that in the future I shall be beginning an article with such a sentence? Possible, sure, but I think unlikely.

For me, one of the most interesting aspects of chess is how people express their personalities through their play. Every player, no matter what their strength, has their own style, their own quirks and idiosyncrasies. Down at your club I'm sure you know a chap who likes to grab material, then retreat behind the barricades waiting to win the ending on the 93rd move — and he invariably works for the Inland Revenue; or the fellow with an insufferable sense of humour who opens 1 b4 in every single game. And that's great. Diversity makes life interesting.

When players with opposing styles, who are well-matched in ability, face each other, the chess struggle can be raised to the level of great art. My favourite World Championship matches were the Tal-Botvinnik encounters of 1960 and 1961. Botvinnik, scientific, steady, rational; seeking to contain the wit, fire and skill of Tal. Wonderful games.

If computers do not have personalities, will anyone be seriously interested in their games? I have heard that there now exists a machine which is programmed to play 'in the style of' Alekhine, Capablanca, or some other past master, according to the flick of a switch. I find that as charmless as a synthesiser's vain attempts to sound like a symphony orchestra.

You might well be wondering what it is that has made me vent my spleen against the silicon monsters. Well, in April 1992 I had a rather unnerving experience at the Neu Isenburg quickplay tournament in Germany. Looking at the pairings on the first day, I spotted another 'King'. Closer examination revealed that this was actually a computer with the name 'King 1.0'. What a scandal: using my name without permission.

This really was too much. I no longer cared about winning the tournament, or preserving my precious Elo points (not much!) — I just had to finish ahead of this adding machine. The family honour was at stake.

In the end, I had to leave the tournament in a hurry - after my performance there, leaving in a hurry seemed like a good idea - so I don't know how it finished, and I haven't been able to find out since. What I do know is that it was a bit too close for comfort ...

Recently there have been several 'Man v. Machine' tournaments, and though the strength of computers is increasing dramatically, they still have a way to go before they will be able to compete at the highest levels in chess. Considering the amount of time which has been invested into developing a computer which can beat the strongest human player - and their failure, as yet, to do so - my faith in the richness and complexity of chess has actually been strengthened.

The game below is from one such event. It gives me the greatest pleasure to be able to present the German Grandmaster Eric Lobron in the role of Luddite, reducing 'Deep Thought 2' to iron filings.

Lobron-Deep Thought 2
IBM Cup, Hannover 1991
Reti Opening

1 ♘f3 d5 2 g3 c6 3 ♗g2 ♗g4 4 c4 e6 5 b3 dxc4 6 bxc4 ♘d7 7 ♗b2 ♕b6 8 ♕c2 ♘gf6 9 0-0 ♗d6 10 d3 0-0

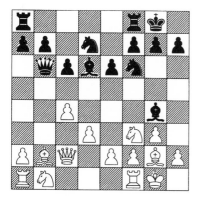

Start predicting human moves now.

11 ♘bd2

Five points. Before embarking on a plan it is best to develop all the pieces. Only one point for 11 ♘c3 which doesn't look quite as harmonious: it is better to keep the bishop's diagonal clear.

11 ... e5

12 ♖ab1

Three points. You can't argue with that one. White places a rook on the open file, and at the same time gains a tempo by threatening a discovered attack on the queen.

12 ... ♕a6

This is the second serious strategic error that Black has made in the game. The first was on the fifth move (5 ... dxc4? voluntarily giving up the centre); and now this. Was the machine lured by that lone a-pawn? Who knows, and who cares. The result is that the queen, thanks to Lobron's careful play, is sidelined for the rest of the game. 12 ... ♕c7 was the natural move.

13 h3

Three points. It does no harm to put the question to the bishop.

13 ... ♗e6

14 ♘g5

Five points. Now that White has completed his development, and with Black's queen conveniently stuck in a corner, the time has come to seize the initiative. 14 d4 (three points) was also a good idea: 14 ... exd4 15 ♘xd4 ♖fe8 16 f4!, threatening f5 and preparing e4, is very dangerous indeed. Note how strong a majority of pawns in the centre can become (5 ... dxc4?).

14 ... ♗f5

15 ♗c3

Three points. Opening the file for the rook. Three points for 15 ♗a1 as well, and indeed the same if you had played either of these on the 13th or 14th moves.

It is tempting to lunge forward in the centre with 15 e4 ♗g6 16 f4, but if Black reacts carefully he will stand well: 16 ... h6! 17 ♘f3 exf4 18 e5 ♗c5+ 19 ♔h1 ♘h5!. White's central

push has been halted and Black is a pawn to the good.

15 ... ♘c5

It probably would have been better to play 15 ... h6 16 ♘ge4 ♘xe4 17 ♘xe4 ♗c7 (17 ... ♗e7 18 ♕b2! hitting b7 and e5) though with his fine pawn structure, pressure on the open file and beautifully posted knight, White holds all the positional trumps.

16 e4

Five points. Here we go.

16 ... ♗g6

17 f4

Four points. The only consistent follow-up.

17 ... exf4

18 gxf4

One point.

18 ... ♘a4

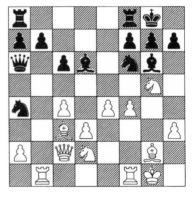

19 ♗a1

Four points. A good move: now

Black has two pieces stranded at the edge of the board. However, if you were consumed with greed and wanted to win a piece with 19 f5, then sadly I'm going to have to reward you with the same number of points (four). It seems a fairly simple matter: 19 f5 ♘xc3 20 ♕xc3 ♗h5 21 e5, and 21 ... ♗c5+ is of course met by 22 d4. Actually Black can just save the piece if he plays 21 ... ♗e7, but the machine's position remains truly miserable after 22 d4.

19 e5 (three points) was also pretty good: 19 ... ♗c5+ 20 ♔h2 ♘d7 21 f5. The pawns sweep everything before them.

19   ...   ♘d7

Not the most challenging continuation. What would your reply have been to 19 ... h6?

It is important to keep the attack going with 20 f5! hxg5 21 e5! (21 fxg6 ♗f4! is still good for White, but not completely clear) 21 ... ♗h5 22 exf6 gxf6 23 ♘e4 or 21 ... ♗xe5 22 ♗xe5 ♗h5 23 ♗xf6! gxf6 24 ♘e4 ♔g7 25 ♖b4! b5 26 cxb5 cxb5 27 ♘g3! hitting the bishop as well as the rook on a8, is a neat variation. If your intention was 20 f5 then take an extra two points, and another one on top of that if you saw 21 e5.

20   e5

Three points. The most straightforward. Only one point for 20 f5 ♗h5.

20   ...   ♗c5+
21   ♔h2

One point. The same for 21 ♔h1.

21   ...   ♗e3
22   ♘ge4

Three points. Once again, the most clear-cut. White continues with his plan of pushing the centre pawns. The threat is f5.

22   ...   ♗xd2
23   ♘xd2

One point and one for 23 ♕xd2 as well. Black would be virtually forced to play 23 ... ♗xe4 24 ♗xe4 which isn't too jolly.

23   ...   ♗f5
24   ♗e4

Three points. Consistent strategy. The blockader of the f-pawn is removed, and so is another defender from around Black's king.

24   ...   ♗xe4
25   ♘xe4

One point.

25   ...   ♘ac5
26   ♘d6

Three points. Everything is winning now. 26 ♘xc5 ♘xc5 27 d4 is also completely bone-crushing (three points).

26   ...   b6
27   ♖g1

Two points. The same score for 27 d4 and 27 f5.

27   ...   g6

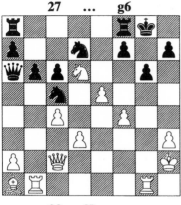

28   f5

Four points. There is really no need to mess around with anything else; a direct assault on the king is clearly going to succeed.

28   ...   ♘b7

29   ♘e4

Three points. Leaving Black's pieces clogged up while heading for the kingside.

29   ...   ♕a3

30   ♕d2

Three points. The decisive switch to the kingside. This was also good on the previous move (three points as well).

30   ...   ♘bc5

31   ♕h6

Two points. The kill. It doesn't require much calculation to see that mate is inevitable — in about three different ways.

31   ...   ♕xa2+

32   ♖g2

Two points. Two for 32 ♖b2 as well, but only one for 31 ♔h1 and 31 ♗b2. The rook moves are more forcing as the queen is attacked.

And here, **Black resigned** (or its operator did the decent thing) as after 32 ... ♕xb1, White can choose between 33 ♘g5 or 33 f6 checkmating.

The late Dutch Grandmaster Jan Hein Donner once said that if he had to play a computer, he would take along a hammer. Judging from this game, we don't need to take such drastic measures ... yet.

10
The Hedgehog

The greatest advance in chess thinking over the past twenty years has been the introduction and development of the Hedgehog system. Anatoly Karpov and Ulf Andersson were the pioneers, using it to score their first tournament successes in the early 1970s. They allowed their opponents to construct a seemingly dominating centre, content to bide their time behind a barricade of pawns. The system came to be known as the Hedgehog, as the tightly packed pawns along the third rank are meant to resemble the animal's dense spines: they give an aggressor a nasty surprise if he gets too close.

And this is exactly what happens in many of the games. Convinced that this large centre gives them the advantage, many players feel the urge to lunge forward, only to find that the greatest damage is done to their own position.

Many Eastern Europeans became adherents of the Hedgehog, notably Zoltan Ribli and Andras Adorjan in Hungary, and Mihai Suba and Florin Gheorghiu in Romania. Suba actually developed a whole philosophy based, for a great part, on the ideas contained within the Hedgehog structure, which he expounds in his provocative and entertaining book *Dynamic Chess Strategy* (Maxwell Macmillan, 1991). This game is typical.

Vukic – Suba
Vinkovci 1977
Hedgehog Defence

1 ♘f3 ♘f6 2 g3 b6 3 ♗g2 ♗b7 4 0-0 e6 5 c4 c5 6 d4 cxd4 7 ♕xd4 d6 8 ♘c3 a6 9 ♖d1 ♕c7 10 b3 ♘bd7 11 ♗b2 ♗e7 12 e4 0-0 13 ♕e3

Now try and predict Black's moves.

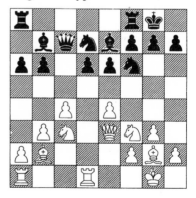

13   ...   ♖fe8

Five points. A strong and subtle move. It is surprising how useful the rook can be when placed opposite the queen, all kinds of tactical possibilities are introduced; more on this later.

14   ♘d4

14   ...   ♗f8

Three points. This 'curling up' is a vital part of Black's strategy in the Hedgehog: on f8 the bishop is safe, well out of the range of White's knights; and the rook on e8 is unmasked.

Supposing White now played 15 f4, how would you reply?

Two points for 15 ... e5. If White captures: 16 fxe5 dxe5 17 ♘f5 ♗c5 wins the queen; and if 16 ♘c2, then 16 ... d5! opening a path for the bishop to go to c5.

This is a good illustration of how Black's position can suddenly, and rather unexpectedly, spring to life, for although they look cramped, Black's forces are actually very well co-ordinated. As Suba puts it, Black's position contains great 'potential energy'.

15   ♖ac1

'A frequent picture in the Hedgehog. White's position looks ideal. That's the naked truth about it, but the "ideal" has by definition one drawback — it cannot be improved.' (Suba's thought-provoking comment on this position.)

Although there is, as yet, no actual contact between the two forces, there is a great deal going on behind the scenes. Did you realise that, as well as being a useful move anyway, 14 ... ♗f8 set up a threat, which 15 ♖ac1 prevented? If White had played 15 h3 instead, what could Black have unleashed?

15 ... d5! (three points) is the move. There is little that can be done to prevent Black isolating the pawn on c4, for if the d-pawn is captured, then the line of the rook is opened up towards the queen: 16 cxd5 exd5, and the e-pawn is as good as lost: or 16 exd5 exd5, and after the queen moves, Black isolates and quickly wins the c-pawn.

15   ...   ♖ad8

Two points. The same score for 15 ... ♖ac8.

With the rook on c1, the d5 break is effectively ruled out: 15 ... d5 16 cxd5 exd5 17 ♘xd5 ♘xd5 18 exd5! ♖xe3 19 ♖xc7 with a winning position.

16   h3

16   ...   g6

Two points. Continuing the regrouping begun by 13 ... ♖fe8.

17   ♔h2

17   ...   ♗g7

One point. The bishop comes to a

more effective diagonal.

18   ♕e2

18   ...   ♕b8

One point. If you played this on any of the previous moves after 15 ... ♖ad8, then take another point. From a tactical point of view, it is very important to bring the queen out of the line of the rook (... d5 is once again threatened, for instance) and indeed, she is no less effectively placed on b8. We have already seen that Black is ready, under the right circumstances, to hit out with ... e5 or ... d5, but the other pawn break that can work to Black's advantage is ... b5, chipping away at the centre. The queen is well placed on b8 to support the b-pawn.

Incidentally, ... d5 is once again threatened, hence White's next move.

19   ♕c2

If instead, White had played 19 f4, how would you have replied?

19 ... e5 (two points) is correct; after 20 fxe5 ♖xe5, Black has tremendous pressure on the e-pawn.

Not, however, 19 ... d5 which looks grim if White plays 20 e5.

19   ...   ♖c8

One point. The shadow boxing continues. Black's rook chases the queen; once again ... d5 is threatened.

Note how Black's pawn breaks must be carefully timed: 19 ... e5, for instance, would have little effect if it doesn't actually open the e-file for the rook. White could just play 20 ♘f3, with the idea of ♘d2-f1-e3, establishing a great clamp on the d5 square.

20   ♕d2
20   ...   ♘c5

Three points. Putting pressure on the e-pawn is a good plan.

20 ... ♖cd8 (two points) keeping the rook opposite the queen as well as supporting the d-pawn is fine, though not quite as active.

21   ♖e1
21   ...   ♕a8

One point. Continuing the assault.

22   f3

In forcing this move, Black has achieved a small, but significant success: the bishop on g2 no longer has influence over the centre; White's second rank no longer has any pawn cover (as we will see later on, when the position opens this can be unpleasant); and a fresh weakness has been created which Black, with his next move, latches onto straightaway.

If White had attempted to avoid this weakness by defending the pawn with 22 ♕e2, what could you play? The typical 22 ... d5! (one point) gives Black a good position: 23 e5 ♘fe4!, and if 24 ♘xe4 dxe4, with the idea of 25 ... ♘d3, is tremendous for Black.

22   ...   ♕b8!

Four points. This is the move to which I alluded in the last note. The queen has achieved her aim on a8, and now shuffles back to b8, whence she eyes up the weak pawn on g3. Beautiful, logical play.

In passing, I should mention that, generally, Black does not need to fear b4 attacking the knight, e.g. 23 b4 ♘cd7 24 ♗f1 ♘e5, and White will have to go into great contortions in order to defend the c-pawn.

23   ♖cd1

23   ...   ♗a8

Two points. Increasing the harmony between Black's pieces. The bishop steps out of the way of the queen, so that she might be able to support the break ... b5.

24   ♘de2

24   ...   ♖ed8

One point. It is best to keep a rook

on the c-file, in case White should have ideas of playing b4.

25   ♘d4

The knight had to return. Why? Supposing White had played 25 ♕e3 instead, what would you have played?

25 ... b5! (two points) is positionally highly desirable; after 26 cxb5 axb5 Black has the better position because of his central pawn majority.

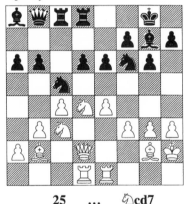

25   ...   ♘cd7

One point. The knight, too, has fulfilled its rôle on c5 and seeks new fields. Nothing for 25 ... d5 because of 26 cxd5 exd5 27 e5.

26   ♕f2

26   ...   ♘e5

One point. In Suba's own words: 'Black starts playing provocatively'. The knight is threatening nothing in particular, but dangling it in front of White's nose when he is unable to do anything about it has got to be good value.

If you just played a waiting move - 26 ... ♖e8, for instance - then take a point. The most important thing is to maintain the harmony in Black's position. Sooner or later White will feel obliged to use his space advantage in some way, by making a rash pawn move perhaps, and then Black will leap out from behind the barricades.

26 ... d5 would still be a mistake: 27 cxd5 exd5 28 exd5 ♘xd5 29 ♘xd5 ♗xd5 30 ♘f5!.

27   ♕e2

27   ...   ♘c6

One point. Playing the knight to this square is slightly unusual, but Suba has a specific idea in mind.

It was still possible to wait: a point for 27 ... ♖e8 or 27 ... ♘ed7.

28   ♘c2

It would have been better for White to play 28 ♘xc6 ♗xc6 29 a4! preventing ... b5 (for the time being).

28   ...   ♘h5!

Five points. The queen on b8 unexpectedly makes it presence felt on the kingside; Black's threat is 29 ... d5, attacking g3. It's extraordinary how this knight move suddenly reveals the weakness of White's kingside — too many pawn moves have been made.

29   f4

29   ...   b5!

Four points. Breakout. The pawn is immune because the knight is pinned.

30   cxb5

30   ...   axb5

One point.

31   ♗f3

31   ...   ♘e7

One point. A point for 31 ... b4 as well, but nothing for 31 ... ♘f6 32 ♘xb5.

32   ♘d4

32   ...   b4

Two points. Driving the knight into exile at the side of the board.

33   ♘a4

33   ...   ♘f6

One point. Having done its job on h5 the knight slips back into the centre, where it supports a potential advance of Black's pawns.

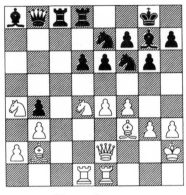

34   e5

White cracks. It is true that Black has the advantage (there is a pleasant choice between breaking with ... e5 or ... d5), but this is disastrous.

34   ...   dxe5

Two points. Much stronger than 34 ... ♗xf3 35 ♘xf3, which gives White the chance to recapture on e5 with a piece.

35   fxe5

If 35 ♗xa8 then 35 ... exd4 36 ♗f3 ♘f5 is beautiful for Black.

35   ...   ♗xf3

One point.

36   ♘xf3

36   ...   ♘fd5

One point. The knight can never be removed from this superb square.

37   ♖c1

37   ...   ♗h6

Three points. The bishop comes to an excellent diagonal, eventually wresting control of the open file.

38   ♖c4

38   ...   ♘e3

One point.

39   ♖cc1

39   ...   ♘7d5

One point.

40   ♖xc8

40   ...   ♖xc8

One point.

41   ♕f2

41   ...   ♘f5

One point.

42   ♖e2

42   ...   ♗e3

One point.

43   ♕e1

43   ...   ♕b5

One point.

44   ♘d2

44   ...   ♕d3

One point.

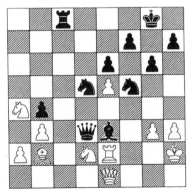

This position represents the triumph of Black's strategy: White was allowed to construct a large, and seemingly strong, pawn centre (rigid and inflexible might be a better description) which Black sniped at from the safety of his own lines, eventually bringing about its destruction. Black's pieces then flooded into the vacuum that was left.

The last shall be first.

45　♘f1

45　...　♖c2

One point. The simplest way to win.

46　♖g2

46　...　♖xg2+

One point.

47　♔xg2

47　...　♛e4+

One point.

White resigned as 48 ♔h2 ♗g1+ wins the queen.

11
Planet Shirov

The Latvian Grandmaster Alexei Shirov is one of the most original attacking players to emerge for decades: sometimes his ideas look as though they could have only come from outer space. I warn you — some of his moves are going to be tough to predict. So, I suggest you imagine that you have been transported to a parallel universe — to Planet Shirov, to be precise.

On Planet Shirov, the weightless atmosphere causes strange things to happen. Chess-pieces float randomly about, their normal, earthly values, a distant memory; in particular, the bishop pair assumes a power unheard of in our solar system.

The alien life-forms that inhabit Planet Shirov are, if only for the unacquainted, a menacing sight: tall and gangly, with tufts of hair that stick out in odd directions, they stumble around, muttering in strange tongues.

Adams-Shirov
Biel 1991
Sicilian Defence
1 e4 c5 2 ♘f3 d6 3 d4 cxd4 4 ♘xd4 ♘f6 5 ♘c3 g6 6 ♗c4 ♗g7 7 0-0 0-0 8 h3 ♘c6 9 ♗e3

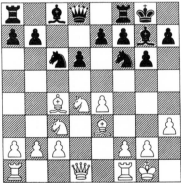

Now imagine that you have been transported to another dimension and start to predict Black's moves.

9   ...   ♘xe4

Five points. No messing around. True to form, Shirov selects the most dynamic continuation, de-stabilising the position. In choosing this move, you would have had to calculate the variation 10 ♘xe4 d5 11 ♘xc6 bxc6 12 ♗d3 (it is best to keep the bishop) 12 ... dxe4 13 ♗xe4, and seen that this position was at least equal for Black; I think the simplest move here is 13 ... ♕c7. Not only is White's queenside a little sensitive, but Black has the natural plan of advancing his kingside majority (... e5, ...f5), at his disposal.

Of course, it was just as good to play the natural developing move, 9 ... ♗d7 (three points), but I have been warning you to 'expect the unexpected', hence the extra points for 9 ... ♘xe4.

10   ♗xf7+

10   ...   ♔xf7!!

Ten points. If you found this move you: (a) are a genius; (b) are a cheat; (c) have a relative languishing in a Latvian gaol.

Let me explain. About five years ago, Alexander Wojtkiewicz, an ethnic Pole living in Latvia, was thrown into prison for evading conscription into the Soviet army. Now, while he was doing his stretch of borscht, he had a lot of time to brood upon Life's great questions, such as, 'Is it possible to rehabilitate the 6 ♗c4 Dragon for Black?'. 10 ... ♔xf7 was the move he came up with. (Previously, 10 ... ♖xf7 - two points if you chose this - had been automatically played, and Black had struggled - it will become clear why in a couple of moves.)

Once out of the clink, being a generous chap, he let a few of his Latvian mates into the secret, and thus Shirov got to hear about it.

11   ♘xe4

11   ...   ♘xd4!

Three points. The only logical follow-up. If your intention was 11 ... ♗d7, allowing 12 ♘g5+ and ♘e6, then deduct five and check your oxygen supply.

11 ... ♔g8 (two points) would at least have the merit of removing the king from the action, but then you may as well have played 10 ... ♖xf7. White could claim a big positional advantage with 12 c4.

12   ♗xd4

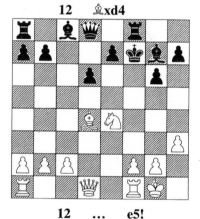

12   ...   e5!

Four points. This is the point of Black's play — he is able to set his centre pawns rolling, backed by the bishop pair. At this point, we can go back and take a look at what would have happened if Black had played 10 ... ♖xf7 and then continued in the same vein: 11 ♘xe4 ♘xd4 12 ♗xd4 e5?, and now 13 ♗c5! d5 14 ♘d6 is virtually winning for White.

Instead of 12 ... e5?, 12 ... ♗f5 was played in the game Stoica-

Makropoulos, Bucharest 1983. The course of the game illustrates the problems Black may face, with hanging pawns on the two central files: 13 ♘g5 ♖f8 14 c4 h6 15 ♗xg7 ♔xg7 16 ♘e4 ♕b6 17 ♕e2 ♗xe 4 18 ♕xe4 ♖f7 19 b3 ♖af8 20 ♕e2 e5 21 ♖ad1 ♖f4 22 ♖d5 e4 23 ♕b2 ♖8f6 24 ♕d4 e3 25 ♕xb6 axb6 26 f3 ♖e6 27 ♖e1 ♖f5 28 ♖xf5 gxf5 29 f4! ♖e4 30 g3 b5! (the best chance, otherwise White's king runs to the centre and takes the e-pawn) 31 cxb5 d5 32 ♔f1 d4 33 ♔e2 ♔f6 34 a4 ♔e6 35 a5 ♔d5 36 a6 bxa6 37 bxa6 ♖e8 38 ♖a1 ♔e4 39 ♖a4 h5 40 a7! ♖a8 41 h4! 1-0. The final position is zugzwang: Black's king must retreat, after which the e- and d-pawns drop. White kept control very well in the final stages.

13 ♗e3

With Black's rook still protecting the queen, 13 ♗c5 is impossible: the point of 10 ... ♔xf7!!. Deep, ha?

13 ... d5

Two points. The only move — and a good one too.

14 ♘g3

I think 14 ♗g5 would be more challenging for Black. Then 14 ... ♕d7 is forced (14 ... ♕a5 15 ♘d6+ ♔g8 16 b4 and ♕xd5+), then 15 ♘c3 forces Black to push again, 15 ... d4 16 ♘e4. This way, at least White has a foothold in the centre. Chances are roughly equal. Take a

couple of points if you saw this idea for White.

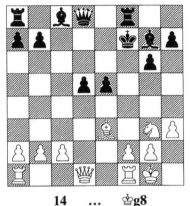

14 ... ♔g8

Four points. A sensible move, tucking the king back into the corner. Only one point for 14 ... d4 — there is no need to give White e4 for the knight. No points for 14 ... ♗e6, which allows White to break up the pawn front with 15 f4!.

15 c3
15 ... ♗e6

Two points.

16 ♘e2
16 ... g5!

Five points. An excellent move. White might even stand better if he gets in f4: after the exchange on e5, he plays ♗d4, if possible, exchanges the bishops, and then plays the knight to d4, or perhaps f4 to hit the d-pawn.

If White is unable to break up the e5, d5 pawn centre, it means that the knight will be unable to find an outpost. As you will see, ultimately, this has fatal consequences.

Of other possible moves, 16 ... ♕d7 (two points) connecting rooks, and perhaps eyeing up a sacrifice on h3, is the most natural. But it does allow 17 f4.

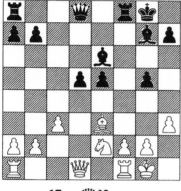

17 ♕d2
17 ... h6

Three points. The best move, but 17 ... g4 (two points) and 17 ... ♗f6 (one point) were reasonable alternatives. Let's take a quick look at these.

A plausible variation after 17 ... g4, is 18 hxg4 ♗xg4 19 f3 ♗e6 20 ♗h6 ♖f7 21 ♗xg7 ♖xg7. Black has a rook on an open file pointing towards the king, but White can take comfort from the exchange of bishops, which weakens the pawn front. Chances are balanced.

17 ... ♗f6 looks awkward. White just keeps up the pressure with 18

♖ad1 ♖f7 19 ♘g3! with the idea of ♘h5.

18 h4
18 ... gxh4

Two points. One point for 18 ... ♗f6 — not bad, but once again, there is something about this move that feels awkward; it doesn't look right to block the rook.

19 ♗xh6

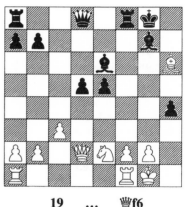

19 ... ♕f6

Three points. The most forceful continuation. Black sacrifices a pawn in order to speed his forces to the kingside.

19 ... ♖f7 (two points), is slower, but still good. The follow-up will be ... ♕f8!, forcing White to make a decision about the bishop, and preparing to bring the queen's rook into play.

Naturally, no points for 19 ... ♗xh6, voluntarily exchanging off the bishop pair and bringing White's queen to a threatening square. In trying to attack, Black has also exposed his own king, so he must proceed with extreme care.

20   ♗g5

Adams accepts the challenge, but exchanging bishops, 20 ♗xg7 ♕xg7, and facing the consequences of 21 f4!? might have been more prudent.

20   ...   ♕g6

One point.

21   ♗xh4
21   ...   ♖f5

Two points.

22   f4

Black's rook was threatening to swing to the h-file, so Adams hits the 'Hyperspace' button. A vain hope: Planet Shirov has been shooting through Hyperspace, at a speed of warp-factor 10, since creation.

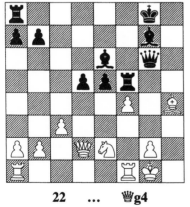

22   ...   ♕g4

Four points. From here on in,

Shirov's calculation is faultless. There were some tempting alternatives: 22 ... ♖h5 (one point), is met by 23 ♗g5!, intending 23 ... ♕h7 24 ♘g3, but 22 ... ♖af8 (two points) is a good try. White has to steer a narrow course, but he should emerge from the mire with the advantage: 23 fxe5! ♗xe5 24 ♖xf5 ♖xf5 25 ♖e1! preparing ♘d4, lining up against the bishops. If 23 ... ♗h6!? then 24 ♕d4; now 24 ... ♖f3!? is a move I would not like to face if short of time, but on reflection, 25 ♖xf3 ♖xf3 26 ♗f2! keeps the advantage.

23   ♗g5

23 g3 is strongly answered by 23 ... ♖h5!; I can't see White lasting long after 24 ♔f2 ♖f8 25 ♔e1 ♗h6.

23   ...   ♖af8

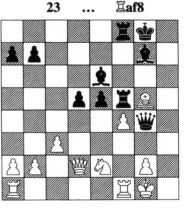

Four points. Bringing the final piece into the attack.

24   ♖f2
24   ...   d4!

Five points. A wonderful move, freeing the bishops.

| 25 | cxd4 |
| 25 | ... | exf4 |

Two points.

| 26 | ♗xf4 |
| 26 | ... | ♗c4 |

Five points. Winning a piece. The knight never made it to a good square.

| 27 | ♗e3 |
| 27 | ... | ♖xf2 |

One point.

| 28 | ♗xf2 |
| 28 | ... | ♗xe2 |

One point. Here **White resigned**. Not one of Adams's greatest performances, but Shirov did play with tremendous energy to net the point.

Postscript: There is a happy ending to Wojtkiewicz's story. After leaving gaol, he managed to emigrate to Poland. In 1990 he achieved the Grandmaster title, and he is now a chess professional.

12
A Theoretical Battle

This game is a typical example of what can happen when a strong, well-prepared player comes up against someone slightly weaker.

The Grünfeld Defence is a very sharp opening indeed and might also be called the 'Grünfeld Counter-Attack'. In true 'Hypermodern' style Black allows White to establish a large centre in the hope that he will be able to then knock it down. It is of course a great gamble, for if he fails, then White's domination of the centre will give him a clear advantage. At the highest levels of chess, one would be ill-advised to essay the opening on a whim.

The two players here, Boris Gelfand from Minsk in White Russia, and Stefan Kindermann from Munich, had in fact already done battle in exactly this variation, the game ending in a draw after some adventures. Both players were, however, dissatisfied with their own handling of the opening and had prepared improvements; but Gelfand's research was the more thorough, and it was he who managed to get his new move in first. Once he secured the advantage his technique in steering the game to victory was most efficient. Kindermann must have felt as though he never had a chance through the whole game.

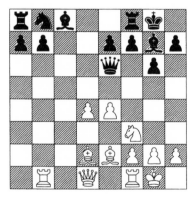

Gelfand-Kindermann
Dortmund 1990
Grünfeld Defence

1 d4 ♘f6 2 c4 g6 3 ♘c3 d5 4 cxd5
♘xd5 5 e4 ♘xc3 6 bxc3 ♗g7 7 ♘f3
c5 8 ♖b1 0-0 9 ♗e2 cxd4 10 cxd4
♕a5+ 11 ♗d2 ♕xa2 12 0-0 ♕e6

Now try predicting White's moves.

13 ♕c2

Four points. There are three reasonable methods of dealing with the threat to the e-pawn: 13 e5, 13 ♗d3 and 13 ♕c2. I would quickly reject 13 e5. It must be a mistake to give Black the chance to occupy the d5 square. 13 ... ♕d5 is a good move, with the idea of ... ♗e6, ... ♕d7, and ... ♗d5. Naturally, White may disrupt the smooth flow of this idea, but the position should be quite satisfactory for Black.

13 ♗d3 (one point) is not bad - it retains some flexibility at least - but 13 ♕c2 is by far the best. The rooks are connected, and White is already contemplating penetration down the open c-file.

13 ... ♕d6

Black must move the queen again in order to develop the bishop on c8.

14 ♗b4

Three points. White brings the bishop to an excellent diagonal with gain of time. The previous Gelfand-Kindermann encounter had continued 14 d5 (one point if you chose this) and now Black should have played 14 ... ♘a6 preventing ♗b4 (I'm sure Kindermann intended this) with a perfectly reasonable position.

Two points for 14 ♖fc1, a sensible move, building up pressure on the c-file.

14 ... ♕d8

15 d5

Three points. In view of the fact that the d-pawn is not protected by another pawn, this move must be played at some point, and since Black threatens ... ♘c6, this is the right moment. Apart from that, it is useful to be able to pin down the e7 pawn, a potential target, as we shall see later in the game.

15 ... ♗g4

16 ♖fc1

Three points. There is already a threat of 17 ♕c7 winning back the pawn with an excellent position.

16 ... ♘a6

17 ♗a3

Two points. Without this bishop White cannot hope to make any significant progress. 17 ♗xa6 would not be good as 17 ... bxa6 18 ♕c7? ♕xc7 19 ♖xc7 allows a nasty pin by 19 ... ♖ab8.

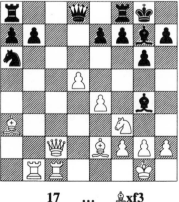

17 ... ♗xf3

18 gxf3

Six points. This undogmatic move is the best of the game. To understand the idea behind it, it is necessary to examine the alternative capture.

Have a consolation point if you played 18 ♗xf3. The b-pawn is still attacked, but in this case Black would be able to play 18 ... b6, with the idea of 19 ... ♘c5. By giving back the pawn in this way Black eliminates the dangerous bishop on a3, and thus achieves some security. The bishop on g7 is a superb piece: if White is not careful it could chaperone the a-pawn right down the board.

After 18 gxf3 it is not possible to defend the b-pawn with ... b6, because the knight would be *en prise*, thus Black is unable to block the bishop on a3. The slight weakness to White's kingside is not significant as he has such a great lead in development.

If Black now played 18 ... ♗h6, how would you respond?

Nothing for the tame 19 ♖d1 allowing 19 ... ♕d7 when Black is holding the position together; 19 ♖xb7! (two points) is correct: 19 ... ♗xc1 20 ♕xc1. White has excellent compensation for the exchange.

18 ... ♕d7

19 ♗xa6

One point.

19 ... bxa6

20 ♕c7

Three points. If the queens are exchanged, the e-pawn drops giving White a winning ending.

20 ... ♕h3

21 ♕g3

Six points. This is an excellent decision. Black is forced to exchange into a miserable endgame, for if 21 ... ♕d7 22 ♖c7 ♕a4 23 ♗xe7 is crushing.

It was tempting to play 21 ♗xe7 (two points). If 21 ... ♕xf3 22 ♗xf8 ♖xf8 23 ♖e1, with the idea ♕g3, should be winning for White. However, if Black plays 21 ... ♖fe8!, then it is surprisingly difficult for White to keep control of the position. If 22 d6 ♗e5! wins; and if 22 ♖b3, defending the f-pawn, then 22 ... ♖ac8 wins a piece. White ought to give back a couple of pawns in order to give his king protection: 22 ♗d6 ♕xf3 23 ♗g3. The d-pawn is still very dangerous, so the position is completely unclear.

21 ... ♕xg3+

22 hxg3

One point. It is best to leave a pawn on f2 so that the king still has protection along the second rank.

22 ... ♖fe8

Black is forced into a position in which both of his rooks are tied down.

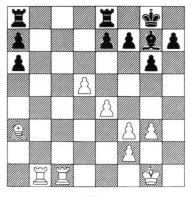

23   ♖b7

One point. The same for 23 ♖c7.

23   ...   ♗f8

If Black had played 23 ... e6, how should White reply?

One point for 24 d6. The pawn will cost Black material.

24   ♖cc7

Two points.

24   ...   ♖ab8

24 ... e5 would at least have complicated the position a little. White has two reasonable moves 25 d6, and 25 ♗b2 (the cleanest move) 25 ... f6 26 ♖xh7 keeps control.

25   ♖xb8

Four points. When one has an advantage in the endgame, one should always be on the look out for continuations which simplify down to a position that is known to be theoretically winning. White keeps the advantage after 25 ♖xa7 (one point), but it cannot be said that the

position is definitely winning; there would be 25 ... ♖b3 and 26 ... ♖xf3 to think about for a start.

25   ...   ♖xb8
26   ♗xe7

Two points. With this Gelfand obtains two extra centre pawns, and experience tells him that this constitutes a winning advantage. Black's a-pawns do not provide sufficient counterplay.

26   ...   ♗xe7
27   ♖xe7

One point.

27   ...   ♖a8
28   ♖c7

Three points. White must take care of the threat to push the a-pawns before advancing his own pawns or bringing up the king.

28 d6 (one point) for instance, might put the win in jeopardy: 28 ... a5 29 ♖e5! (the only move to keep winning chances; if 29 d7 ♔f8 30 ♖e5 ♖d8 31 ♖d5 ♔e7 wins the d-pawn and secures at least a draw) 29 ... ♖d8 30 ♖d5! f6 31 f4! with the idea of e5, protecting the d-pawn, followed by ♖xa5.

In the above variations, White has to find a string of exact moves in order to keep on the winning path. Gelfand's method is very much simpler: there is really no need to push any pawns until the rest of the position is secure.

28   ...   a5

29   ♖c5

Three points.

29   ...   a4

30   ♖a5

One point.

30   ...   ♔f8

31   e5

Two points. The same for 31 f4.

31   ...   ♔e7

32   f4

Three points. As well as strengthening the centre, this rules out the possibility of Black playing ... g5 and ... h5, creating another passed pawn.

32   ...   h5

It would have been a little more testing for Black to have marched his king across to try to clear a path for the passed a-pawn, though White wins if he keeps his nerve and plays as in the game.

33   ♔g2

Two points.

33   ...   a3

34   ♔f3

Three points. There is really no need to capture the pawn yet, it is better just to advance the king.

34   ...   a2

35   ♔e4

One point.

35   ...   a1(♕)

36   ♖xa1

One point.

36   ...   a5

37   ♖a4

Three points. The pawn should be halted as quickly as possible.

37   ...   ♖a7

38   f5

Three points. **Black resigned** here before he was rolled off the board by White's centre pawns.

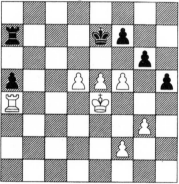

A smooth performance, but only because Gelfand's play was so incisive. There were two moves which were particularly fine. First, 18 gxf3 was easy to overlook — I suspect Kindermann did so when he was considering this position a few moves before. Also 21 ♕g3 was a difficult move to find, since it would have been necessary to see that after the obvious capture on e7, Black would have gained excellent counterplay, and then, when one had found 21 ♕g3, the resulting ending would have to be accurately assessed.

13
Brick-walls

Being a second is often a nerve-racking business. You prepare your player as best you can for each of his opponents, but when the game begins there is nothing more that you can do. One is forced to watch events unfolding on the board with frustrating impotence. The best thing to do is escape from the tournament hall: anxiousness can translate itself — and not just to one's own player. Parents take note! Having said that, it is hard to resist taking a look now and again to see how things are going.

In this respect, seconding Michael Adams in the World Under-16s in 1987 was certainly one of my worst experiences. The games followed a regular pattern: after about two hours he would be grovelling around on the back rank, his pieces forced into terrible contortions. I would exit and try to soothe my nerves by taking a coffee and ice-cream in front of Innsbruck's Goldener Dach. On returning at the end of the fourth hour, Michael's pieces would unerringly have found their way to rock-solid squares, and his opponent would look like a man who had spent the entire afternoon beating his head against a brick-wall. All's well that ends well, but did I go through hell in the first few hours of each game.

Since then, Michael Adams has fulfilled the great promise which he showed in those days, though one still could not describe him as a great opening theoretician: it is very often his great natural talent which pulls him through.

His opponent here is Grandmaster Alexander Khalifman from Leningrad.

Khalifman-Adams
Groningen 1990
Bogo-Indian Defence

1 d4 ♘f6 2 c4 e6 3 ♘f3 ♗b4+ 4 ♗d2 ♕e7 5 g3 ♘c6 6 ♘c3 ♗xc3 7 ♗xc3 ♘e4 8 ♖c1 d6 9 ♗g2 ♘xc3 10 ♖xc3

Now start setting up a brick-wall for Black.

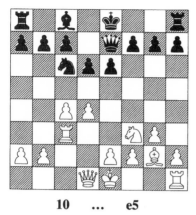

10   ...   e5

Four points. Black must stake a claim in the centre, and this is the right way to do it. 10 ... d5, on the other hand, would not be good: the bishop remains blocked in, and White obtains automatic play on the c-file. Instead 10 ... f5 is plausible, transposing into a kind of Dutch Defence, but not really very good if White reacts swiftly: 11 d5! ♘e5 12 ♘d4!. The best alternative is the sensible 10 ... 0-0 (two points), but White might cut across Black's plans with 11 d5!.

11   d5
11   ...   ♘b8

Two points. This is the best retreat. From d8 the knight might crawl out via f7 eventually, but it looks tortuous.

12   0-0
12   ...   0-0

Two points. Necessary evacuation.

13   ♘d2

13   ...   a5

Four points. If Black begins kingside operations with 13 ... f5 (one point), he is liable to get hammered on the queenside before the attack starts in earnest: after 14 b4! White already threatens c5.

14   c5
14   ...   ♘a6!

Four points. Typical Adams. Instead of getting embroiled in the complications that would ensue if he grabbed the pawn, he prefers to continue with his own steady scheme. In fact, it is quite possible to accept the pawn: 14 ... dxc5!? (two points) 15 ♘b3 ♘a6 (15 ... b6? 16 d6!) 16 ♕c1! ♘b4 17 ♖xc5 ♘xa2 18 ♕c4. After the c-pawn falls White must be better, but Black is not without counter-chances.

15   cxd6
15   ...   cxd6

One point. Deduct two if you recaptured with the queen, creating a chronic weakness in the form of your c7 pawn.

16   ♘c4
16   ...   ♕d8

Three points. Another retreat, and another good move. In addition to protecting the a-pawn, the queen covers the b6 square. The natural 16 ... ♘c5 (sorry, no points) would not, however, be so bright: 17 ♖a3! with the secondary threat of b4, wins a pawn and drives the knight from c5. Add another point if you spotted this powerful move.

17   a3

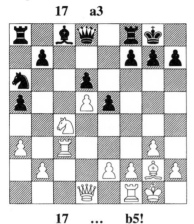

17   ...   b5!

Four points. Seizing the initiative on the queenside. Once more, 17 ... ♘c5 would not be a good move: 18 b4 axb4 19 axb4 ♘a4 20 ♖a3! b5 21 ♘a5 heading for c6, is to White's advantage.

18   ♘d2
18   ...   ♗d7

Two points. A steady follow-up, connecting the 'heavy pieces' on the back rank.

19   ♕b1
19   ...   b4

Three points. Take a couple of points if this was your choice on the last move. This is the most forceful way to proceed. If Black makes another developing move, say 19 ... ♕b6!? (two points), then 20 b4! halts further queenside expansion.

Even this position seems a little better for Black though: White's b-pawn is weak while Black's position is like granite.

20   axb4
20   ...   axb4

Two points. Only one point for 20 ... ♘xb4 which gives White time to breathe.

21   ♖cc1
21   ...   ♘c5

Two points. If you envisaged, from the time that you played 11 ... ♘b8 and 13 ... a5, that the knight would end up on this square, then take three bonus points. This knight is the linchpin of Black's position and without it the structure would fall apart. From here on White is in trouble: there is nothing he can attack, and Black can calmly bring up the reserves.

22   ♘e4
22   ...   ♗f5!

Two points. It is essential that the knight is maintained on c5, so deduct a point if your choice was 22 ... ♘xe4 exchanging off Black's best piece.

23   ♖c4
23   ...   b3

Three points. The hasty 23 ... ♗xe4? would leave Black with a rotten position after 24 ♗xe4, when both h- and b-pawns are attacked. There is only one way to save the pawn: 24 ... ♘xe4 25 ♕xe4 f5 26 ♕c2 when White's control of the c-file gives him a clear advantage. Now you see how important it is to keep that knight. Likewise 23 ... ♕b6?? (deduct five) would not be too clever: 24 ♘f6+ spoils a lot of good work. Finally 23 ... ♖b8 (one point) is sensible, but uninspired.

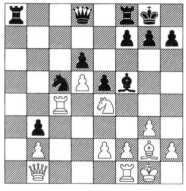

| 24 | ♕c1 |
| 24 | ... | ♗xe4 |

Two points. No points for others — this is a forced move.

| 25 | ♗xe4 |
| 25 | ... | f5 |

Two points.

| 26 | ♗g2 |
| 26 | ... | ♕a5 |

Two points. It is time to bring the heavy artillery into the game. Also two for 26 ... ♕b6. Take two points instead if you wanted to play either of these on the previous move. Now that the knight is firmly entrenched,

it is not quite so necessary to be precise with the order of moves.

| 27 | h4 |

Evidence that White has no constructive plan at his disposal.

| 27 | ... | ♕b5 |

Four points. A fine 'creeping' move, to use Kotov's terminology. The queen hits some sensitive spots in White's position and prepares to use the rook on the a-file.

| 28 | ♕c3 |

| 28 | ... | ♘a4! |

Three points. Forcing simplification into a winning endgame. There are other good moves in the position: two points for 28 ... ♖a2 and 28 ... ♖a4.

| 29 | ♕b4 |
| 29 | ... | ♕xb4 |

One point.

| 30 | ♖xb4 |
| 30 | ... | ♖fb8 |

Two points. The clearest. 30 ... ♘c5 (one point) allows White a hint of counterplay with 31 ♖b6.

31 ♖xb8+

31 ... ♖xb8

One point.

32 ♖b1

32 ... ♖c8

Three points. Grabbing the open file. One for 32 ... ♔f7, but the rook move is much more to the point.

33 ♗h3

33 ... g6

One point.

34 e4

34 ... ♖c2

One point.

35 ♖a1

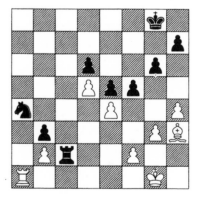

35 ... ♘c5!

Three points. 35 ... ♘xb2 (one point) is winning too, but moving the knight back to its optimal post is the most efficient, not to mention the most elegant, way to decide the game.

36 exf5

36 ... ♖xb2

One point. It would be a mistake to allow White's bishop into the game with 36 ... gxf5.

37 fxg6

37 ... hxg6

One point.

38 ♗e6+

38 ... ♔f8

Two points. Taking the bishop complicates matters unnecessarily: 38 ... ♘xe6 39 dxe6 ♖a2 40 ♖b1 b2 41 ♔g2 and White is still kicking. A point for 38 ... ♔g7 which should be about the same as the game assuming that it was not your intention to answer 39 ♖a7+ with 39 ... ♔f6.

39 ♖a8+

39 ... ♔e7

One point. Here **White lost on time**, but in any case there is not a great deal he can do to stop the b-pawn.

14
Classical Originality

The more I look at Vassily Ivanchuk's games, the more I believe that he could become the strongest player in the world. Although essentially a classical player, Ivanchuk's games often have a touch of originality to them which marks him out, even at the highest level, as being special. His style is very much in contrast to the pragmatism of the 1970s and early 1980s in that he strives to find the truth in a position, rather than play a move which just 'looks' good.

Unlike most top players, Ivanchuk does not specialise in a couple of favourite openings, as for instance Kasparov does with the King's Indian and the Najdorf, but instead plays a whole variety of systems. (Computer databases enable one to take in a great deal of information very quickly, so this may be a growing trend.) Having said that, one could not accuse him of being a slave to theory as he discovers so many new ideas in the opening.

Note how in the first sentence I said 'could' become the strongest player in the world. He has perhaps one fatal flaw: poor nerves. The most tragic case of this was his failure to clinch victory in his Candidates match against Yusupov in 1991. If he could overcome this weakness, I believe he would make it to the top. It is a very big 'if', though.

Ivanchuk's opponent in this game is an International Master from Spain.

Ivanchuk - Pomes
Terrassa 1991
Dutch Defence

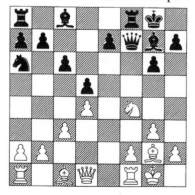

1 d4 f5 2 g3 ♘f6 3 ♗g2 g6 4 ♘h3 ♗g7 5 ♘f4 0-0 6 0-0 ♕e8 7 ♘c3 c6 8 e4 fxe4 9 ♘xe4 ♘xe4 10 ♗xe4 d5 11 ♗g2 ♘a6 12 c3 ♕f7

Start predicting White's moves now.

13 ♘d3

Five points. The objectives for both sides are clear: White is attempting to control and then occupy the square in front of Black's 'backward' e-pawn; Black would like to effect the pawn break ... e5, which would leave him with a greater share of the centre due to the strong pawn on d5. In this context, the knight move makes total sense.

For a developing move such as 13 ♗e3, no points, as Black may play 13 ... e5! 14 dxe5 ♗xe5, liberating his position. 13 ♖e1 is better motivated, but I wouldn't consider this move on principle: with Black's queen and rook lined up against f2 it simply looks too risky to leave its protection (no points).

13 ♕e2 (one point) is not bad.

13 ... ♗f5
14 ♗f4

Three points. Black had renewed his strategic threat. If for instance 14 ♕e2, then 14 ... ♗xd3 15 ♕xd3 e5. The only other method of preventing ... e5 was 14 f4, but this is heavy-handed. The bishop on c1 is blocked in, and some key white squares (e4, g4) weakened. All the same, one point.

14 ... g5
15 ♘e5

Three points. The most consistent continuation, keeping control over the e5 square.

Two points for 15 ♗e5, which would be wonderful if Black played 15 ... ♗xe5 16 ♘xe5, giving White total control, but 15 ... ♗xd3 is correct: 16 ♕xd3 ♗xe5 17 dxe5. Black no longer has any problems down the e-file, but his king is a little exposed. The position is unclear.

Deduct two for 15 ♗xg5 which loses a piece after 15 ... ♕g6.

15 ... ♗xe5
16 ♗xe5

One point.

16 ... ♕g6

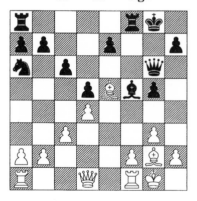

17 g4

Six points. An extraordinary move. White has already secured a pleasant advantage (just look at the uncontested bishop on e5), and could have quite reasonably continued with moves such as 17 ♕d2 or 17 ♖e1 (two points for both) preparing to build up pressure on the e-file; in other words it would have been quite in order for White to switch on to automatic pilot, to play all the standard moves without much thought.

But Ivanchuk is still looking to play the most exact move in the position. He realises that Black's best piece is the bishop on f5, and indeed if it can be cemented there with moves such as ... g4, ... h5, and ... e6, it will make White's task of breaking through on the kingside difficult; hence 17 g4 dislodging the bishop. White can get away with playing a pawn up in front of his king because the bishop on e5 controls so many important squares.

Of other moves, 17 ♕b3 (three points) is the best. The only way to protect the b-pawn is 17 ... b6, which looks extremely ugly.

17	...	♗e4
18	♗xe4	

Three points. Ivanchuk prefers to keep the momentum going rather than play 18 f3 (one point) which also isn't bad. However in this case, Black would have a little more time to regroup his pieces: 18 ... ♗d3 19 ♖e1 ♘b8! 20 ♖e3 (20 ♗xb8 ♖axb8 21 ♖xe7 ♖fe8 with good compensation for the pawn) 20 ... ♗a6 21 ♕d2 ♘d7 22 ♖ae1 ♖f7 23 ♗g3 ♕g7. Black has managed to hold his position together and threatens ... ♘f8-g6-f4.

18	...	♕xe4
19	♖e1	

Three points. The queen must be driven out.

19	...	♕g6
20	♕b3	

Four points. The most forceful continuation. It is important that the rooks are connected, and White achieves this with gain of time; moreover, defending the b-pawn is awkward.

20 ♖e3 (two points) with the simple idea of ♕e2 and ♖e1 is also strong.

20	...	♕f7
21	f4	

Four points. Obviously foreseen when playing 20 ♕b3. The only decent alternative was 20 ♗g3 (one point) but such a miserable retreat is not in the spirit of 20 ♕b3.

21	...	e6

The pawn on b7 had to be defended: if instead 21 ... gxf4 22 ♕xb7 f3 23 ♔f2! puts a stop to Black's kingside activity; and then the knight on a6 cannot be saved.

22	♖f1

Two points. Saving the pawn and at the same time bringing the rook to the open file.

22	...	gxf4
23	♖xf4	

One point.

23	...	♛d7
24	♖af1	

Two points.

24	...	♖xf4
25	♖xf4	

One point.

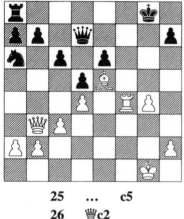

25	...	c5
26	♛c2	

Three points. The queen has served its purpose on b3, and now looks towards Black's open kingside. The same for 26 ♛d1. Deduct two for 26 dxc5, which only brings back the knight into play: 26 ... ♘xc5 and next 27 ... ♘e4; the whole game has turned.

26	...	cxd4
27	g5	

Five points. Another energetic move. If it had been Ivanchuk's intention simply to recapture on d4, then he would have put the queen on d1: 27 cxd4 ♖c8 gains a useful tempo. One point for 27 cxd4 anyway.

Instead 27 ♗xd4 (one point) looks terribly strong at first sight. White threatens to bring the queen into the attack (via e2 and e5 for instance), and there seems to be little that Black can do to prevent it; exchanging rooks doesn't help as the a-pawn is *en prise*. In fact, 27 ... ♘b8!! gives Black good chances to defend the position; from c6 the beast will attack the bishop and control the e5 square.

27	...	♖f8

If 27 ... dxc3 28 g6 rips open the kingside.

28	♖xf8+	

One point.

28	...	♔xf8
29	cxd4	

One point.

29	...	♛c6
30	♛xc6	

Four points. An excellent decision. To understand why White exchanged queens it is first necessary to appreciate just what his advantages are in this position. First, he has the better minor piece: Black's knight is trapped at the side while the bishop dominates from the centre of the board. Second, White may easily create a passed pawn on the kingside; as Black's extra centre pawn is blocked, in effect, this means that White is a pawn up. By exchanging queens, White reduces the position down to just these elements, and this is sufficient to force a win.

30 ♕f2+ (one point) was tempting, but not quite as clean. If Black plays 30 ... ♚e8, then he avoids getting mated and can look forward to gaining some counterplay with his queen.

Nothing for 30 ♕xh7 ♕c1+ 31 ♚f2 ♕xg5 with counterplay.

30 ... bxc6

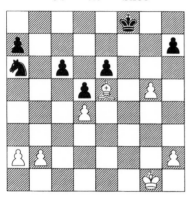

31 h4

Three points. Setting the majority in motion.

31 ... ♚f7

32 ♗d6

Four points. The crucial move. The knight is completely dominated.

32 ... ♚g6

33 ♚f2

One point. The same for 33 ♚g2.

33 ... e5

A desperate attempt to break

White's bind. How would you have played in reply to 33 ... ♚f5 instead?

34 b4 (one point) is correct, with the idea of a4 and b5 winning the knight.

34 dxe5

One point. More forcing than 34 ♗xe5.

34 ... ♚f5

If 34 ... c5 then 35 e6.

35 b4

One point. The same for 35 ♚f3. After 35 ... c5 36 a3 d4 37 b3, Black runs out of moves so must retreat his king, and the game is lost: if 37 ... ♚e6 38 h5; and if 37 ... ♚g6 38 e6.

35 ... c5

36 ♗xc5

One point. Much simpler than 36 bxc5 ♘b4, and Black holds out for a little longer.

36 ... ♚xe5

The king and pawn ending is lost: 36 ... ♘xc5 37 bxc5 ♚xe5 38 h5 and Black cannot stop both passed pawns.

37 a3

Two points. A cool move. The bishop still cannot be captured, so the win of a second pawn is ensured.

37 ... ♘c7

38 ♗xa7

One point.

38 ... ♘b5

39 ♗b8+

One point.

39	**...**	**♔e4**
40	**h5**	

One point. Passed pawns should be pushed; particularly when they can't be caught.

40	**...**	**♘d4**

If 40 ... ♔f5 41 g6 hxg6 42 h6 ♔f6 43 ♗e5+ ♔xe5 44 h7.

41	**g6**

One point. Here **Black resigned** as after 41 ... hxg6 42 h6, the pawn cannot be stopped.

15
The Greatest Fighter

Samuel Reshevsky died on April 4 1992, aged eighty. He must have had the longest professional playing career of any chessplayer — seventy-five years. Born in Poland, he toured Europe as a child prodigy giving simultaneous displays; and he was playing actively right up to his death.

Reshevsky played, and figured prominently, in some of the greatest tournaments in chess history: 3rd-5th Nottingham 1936; 3rd-4th in the World Championship tournament of 1948; equal 2nd in the Zurich Candidates 1953; tied 1st with Korchnoi at Buenos Aires 1960 ahead of a dozen Grandmasters, including Bobby Fischer; and US champion on numerous occasions — the last time being in 1984 at the age of 73.

He had a tremendous match record. He beat Najdorf twice, in 1952 and 1953, and Gligoric in 1952, to confirm his status of 'Best in the West'; and then there was the infamous match with Fischer in 1961, abandoned at 5-5 after a dispute.

In individual encounters, he defeated seven world champions: Lasker, Capablanca, Alekhine, Euwe, Botvinnik, Smyslov, and Fischer. This list alone attests to his remarkable consistency and longevity.

David Bronstein, in a talk he gave to some English juniors a couple of years ago, singled out Reshevsky as the greatest fighter he had ever known. He would always play to win: draw offers were only made for psychological effect when he was worse. Reshevsky's determination, enabling him to fight back from dubious positions, or to strive against the odds for a win, was undoubtedly his greatest strength; but paradoxically, it was also the root cause of his greatest weakness: time-trouble.

In his superb book on the 1953 Candidates tournament, Bronstein (again) makes some revealing comments. Reshevsky is playing Euwe and has just made a risky pawn grab: 'Not everyone would decide to take such a pawn … But Reshevsky is prepared, if he sees a chance to win, to think it over for two hours and twenty-five minutes, if it means he will then be able to exploit that chance and fashion a win out of it.' He went on to win the game.

Reshevsky's tremendous competitiveness sometimes led to what one might call 'gamesmanship'. Again, I quote from Bronstein, commenting on the game Reshevsky-Kotov, Candidates 1953.

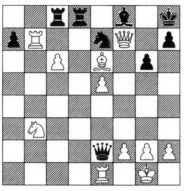

Kotov, in a lost position, has found a great swindle. His last move was 34 ... ♛d3-e2!; now if 35 ♖f1 ♖d1 36 ♘d2 ♛xd2. Bronstein describes the scene marvellously: 'Reshevsky seized his head in his hands, glanced nervously at his flag (ready to fall at any moment) and the position, and took the bishop with check. Then Reshevsky asked how many moves had been made (which is not acceptable grandmaster practice), and received an answer from one of the spectators (which is really illegal).' Reshevsky made the time control, and Kotov duly resigned.

His tenacity and fighting spirit hardly diminished with age. I first met him at the Reykjavik Open in 1984 which was, in the nicest possible way, an incredibly bloodthirsty event. He came equal first. I have a lasting memory of the closing ceremony, when the first prize-winners, Reshevsky, Jon Arnason and Johann Hjartarson, stood on the platform to a thunderous ovation. The two tall Icelanders standing on either side of the diminutive Sammy, patting a shoulder each, made a comical but rather touching picture.

Even a month before his death he played in a veterans' tournament in Moscow, followed by a short match with Smyslov. The result: 2-2, all the games were decisive.

The game I've chosen is from the World Championship tournament 1948, which Botvinnik, his opponent here, went on to win. It is a typically gritty struggle from Reshevsky.

Botvinnik-Reshevsky
World Championship tournament,
Moscow 1948
Nimzo-Indian Defence

**1 d4 ♘f6 2 c4 e6 3 ♘c3 ♗b4 4 e3
c5 5 a3 ♗xc3+ 6 bxc3 ♘c6 7 ♗d3
0-0 8 ♘e2 b6 9 e4**

Now try and predict Black's moves.

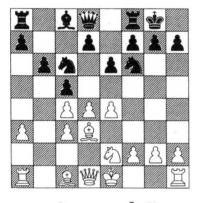

9   ...   ♘e8!

Four points. A difficult move to start with.

9 ... d6 (one point) is a solid move — but fails to sense the coming danger. Take for example, the continuation of the game Gligoric-Lokvenc, 1949: 10 0-0 ♗a6 11 f4 ♘a5 12 f5! ♘d7 (12 ... ♗xc4 13 ♗g5! is a lethal pin) 13 f6! gxf6 14 ♗h6 with a winning attack. Or alternatively, 10 ... ♘e8 11 f4 ♗a6 12 f5 e5 13 f6! ♔h8 14 d5 ♘a5 15 ♘g3, and White's attack came to a

swift conclusion in the famous game Bronstein-Najdorf, Budapest 1950.

From these fragments, we can see both sides' objectives: White is trying to blast open lines on the kingside for his bishops and heavy pieces; Black is aiming at the weak c4 pawn, which is virtually indefensible after ... ♗a6 and ... ♘a5. Black's problem is that even if his strategy succeeds, he might well lose the game. So at some point, a little containment is going to be necessary on the kingside.

10   ♗e3
10   ...   d6

One point. The most natural looking move, but it might be even better just to leave the pawn hanging and carry on with the standard plan. For instance: 10 ... ♗a6 (two points) 11 dxc5 bxc5 12 ♗xc5 d6 13 ♗d4 ♕a5 14 0-0 ♘e5 15 ♗xe5 dxe5, and White's queenside pawns are not long for this world. Naturally, White ought not to take on c5, but then again, that proves that ... d6 is not strictly necessary. 10 ... ♘a5 is also possible (two points); the continuation of the game Lehmann-Janata, 1969, similarly shows that it is worth sacrificing a pawn for the initiative: 11 dxc5 ♕c7 12 cxb6 axb6 13 c5 bxc5 14 0-0 ♗a6 with an excellent position.

No points for 10 ... cxd4: this gives White the possibility to solve the problem of his c-pawn with a timely c5 advance.

11 0-0

11 ... ♘a5

Two points for this or for 11 ... ♗a6 carrying out the standard Nimzo-Indian plan of attacking c4. Black has another plan at his disposal: 11 ... e5, blocking the centre pawns, and thus limiting the scope of White's bishops. Compared to other lines in the Nimzo, I'm not sure this idea is quite as good here: White is already able to push the f-pawn; so only one point.

12 ♘g3

12 ... ♗a6

One point. There is no reason to be distracted from the task.

13 ♕e2

13 ... ♕d7

Three points. A multi-purpose move. The most obvious idea is to play the queen to a4, to increase the pressure against c4. 13 ... ♖c8 (intending ... cxd4 and ... ♗xc4) would not be so good: White closes the centre with 14 d5 and is all set to charge the f-pawn down the board.

13 ... cxd4 (one point) is interesting: 14 cxd4 ♖c8 15 ♖ac1, but there is no decent follow-up.

14 f4

The moment of truth has arrived. How are you going to deal with the advance of the f-pawn?

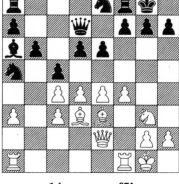

14 ... f5!

Five points. This has been Reshevsky's intention since he played 9 ... ♘e8. (Incidentally, this was the other main idea behind 13 ... ♕d7 — to support f5.) With the pawn securely blockaded on f4, the scope of White's bishops is severely restricted.

14 ... ♕a4 is very risky indeed. After 15 f5! Black has every chance of getting massacred. If this was your intention, I'll give you a point for your courage.

15 ♖ae1

15 ... g6

Two points. It is necessary to buttress f5; White was preparing d5. Deduct two points if you exchanged on e4 or d4. I have already said enough about the need to keep those bishops (and the rest of White's pieces) blocked in behind the pawns. These moves would only release all that pent-up energy.

16   ♜d1

Of course, it would have been better to have played this last move.

16   ...   ♕f7

Two points. A very prudent move. As soon as the rook comes opposite the queen, it is time to shift. 16 ... ♕a4 (one point) would have been rather careless: 17 d5! ♗xc4 (17 ... exd5 18 exf5! wrecks Black's kingside) 18 dxe6 ♗xe6 19 exf5 ♗xf5 and now whichever way White captures on f5, he has good attacking chances for the pawn; Black's queen has strayed too far from the kingside.

17   e5

How would you have responded to 17 d5 here?

Have another point for 17 ... ♘g7! then if 18 e5 ♜ad8! — there is no need to exchange yet, indeed Black might even make another preparatory move, ... ♜fe8, before demolishing the centre; White can do nothing. An instructive variation.

Capturing either pawn would have been a gross error: 17 ... exd5 18 exf5, destroying Black's kingside; 17 ... fxe4 18 ♘xe4 exd5 19 cxd5 ♗xd3 20 ♕xd3 threatening ♘e4-g5-e6, is painful.

17   ...   ♜c8

Two points. No points for 17 ... dxe5? 18 fxe5! opening the bishop's diagonal to h6 and allowing White the possibility of ♘e4!?. 17 ... cxd4? is also bad: 18 ♗xd4! is very

dangerous.

18   ♜fe1

18   ...   dxe5!

Three points. Exactly the right moment. If, despite my repeated warnings, you grabbed the c-pawn, 18 ... cxd4 19 ♗xd4 ♗xc4?? 20 exd6 and ♕e5, then deduct five. Instead of 19 ... ♗xc4??, 19 ... ♘c6! is not a bad move (two points if this was your intention) 20 exd6 ♘xd4 21 cxd4 ♘xd6, which is roughly equal.

19   dxe5

If 19 fxe5 then it would have been safe, at last, to take the c-pawn: 19 ... cxd4 20 cxd4 ♗xc4!.

19   ...   ♘g7

Two points. The most sensible move, connecting the two rooks.

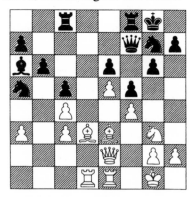

Let's take stock. Reshevsky has clearly won the opening battle: the kingside attack has been well and truly thwarted; the centre is blocked making White's bishops impotent; and what's more, Black still has chronic pressure against c4. Is this a winning position for Black? If White is complacent, yes; but Botvinnik finds a good way to regroup his pieces.

20   ♘f1!

20   ...   ♖fd8

One point.

21   ♗f2

21   ...   ♘h5!

Three points. Out of the blue, White was threatening to activate a bishop. On the h4-d8 diagonal it would be very effective, preventing Black from doubling on the d-file, and if the position ever broke open, it could be troublesome floating around Black's king. Threatening the f-pawn effectively prevents the manoeuvre. No points for other moves — this was a serious threat.

22   ♗g3

White could have returned to e3, but that would have been an admission of defeat. This is better as the knight can move to e3, giving vital protection to c4.

Instead 22 g3 was highly undesirable. Why?

The weakness on the long diagonal would be highly unpleasant for White; it doesn't take too much effort for Black to set up a battery with queen and bishop. Another point if

you noticed this.

22   ...   ♕e8

Two points. Returning to the old plan.

23   ♘e3

23   ...   ♕a4!

Two points. There is no need to exchange off the bishop yet. For instance: 23 ... ♘xg3 24 hxg3 ♕a4 25 g4! and White would have serious counterplay.

24   ♕a2

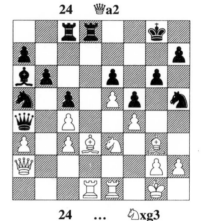

24   ...   ♘xg3

One point. Now that the queen has moved from e2, the bishop was once again threatening to move to h4. There was one other move that cuts across White's plan. Were any of you mad enough to think of 24 ... g5 here? This is just the kind of move that makes me despair as a chess coach. You spend half a day enthusing about Black's deep Nimzo-Indian strategy and then your pupil chucks away everything with a cheap two-mover. The idea is, naturally, 25 fxg5 f4 winning a piece. As well as all the tempting sacrifices, White could simply play 25 ♕f2 to support f4. Black's king is very bare.

25   hxg3
25   ...   h5

Two points. An understandable decision. Reshevsky is worried about White playing g4, and therefore closes the kingside. However, this allows Botvinnik a drawing opportunity. He could have now played 26 ♗c2 and if 26 ... ♕c6 27 a4! shuts out the queen permanently; 26 ... ♗xc4 fails to 27 ♗xa4 ♗xa2 28 ♗d7 ♖b8 29 c4! ♔f7 30 ♖d6 and e6 falls.

In view of this, Keres, in his notes to this game, recommends forcing a queen exchange instead: 25 ... ♕b3 26 ♕xb3 ♘xb3, but to me this seems far too dangerous for Black: 27 g4! ♘a5 28 gxf5 gxf5 29 g4! fxg4 30 f5!; or 27 ... fxg4 28 ♘xg4 ♘a5 29 ♘f6+ ♔g7 30 ♘e4! and ♘d6. So only one point for 25 ... ♕b3.

26   ♗e2?

Now Black is on course once more.

26   ...   ♔f7

One point.

27   ♔f2
27   ...   ♕b3

Four points. This is the important move, and really it should been have

played on the last turn (four more if you did just that). Going for the ending is the only way to make progress.

28   ♕xb3
28   ...   ♘xb3

One point.

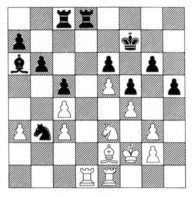

29   ♗d3

Supposing White had just waited here and played 29 ♘f1 (stopping ♘d2), how would you make progress? Black has a very deep plan, so take your time trying to find it.

The winning plan can be neatly divided into stages:

1. Put the knight on a5, forcing White to play ♘e3.

2. Move the king to e7 and exchange off all the rooks on the d-file.

3. March the king to h6 and play g5.

4. Play the knight into b3, and if possible d2 and e4. If White brings his king across to stop this incursion, then h4 will open the way for Black's king. Because White's pieces are tied to the defence of c4, there is nothing that can be done to prevent the scheme's execution.

Award yourself a point for each stage that you saw, to a maximum of four.

29 ... &e7

No points for this move! One point for 29 ... ♘a5 keeping White on the defensive.

30 &e2

30 ... ♘a5

One point.

31 ♖d2

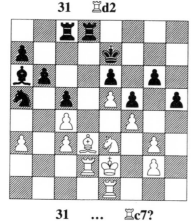

31 ... ♖c7?

No points for this move either. In severe time pressure, Reshevsky overlooks a tremendous counter-shot. When one's opponent is almost bound hand and foot, it is very easy to relax one's guard, imagining that the point is already in the bag. I'm sure this is part of the explanation for the oversight, not just Reshevsky's habitual time shortage.

If you had seen the following pawn sacrifice, and played 31 ... &f7, retracting Reshevsky's 29th, then take five points. The win would then be rather easy: double on the d-file and something is bound to drop (perhaps with a little encouragement, ... &a6- b7-c6-a4 for instance — I'm assuming the rook is on d1.)

32 g4!

A brilliant resource.

32 ... ♖cd7

Two points. A point for both 32 ... hxg4 33 ♖h1! with good counterplay down the h-file; and 32 ... fxg4 33 &xg6 with good drawing chances.

33 gxf5

33 ... gxf5

One point. Naturally not 33 ... &xc4 34 f6+! &f7 35 ♖ed1.

34 ♖ed1

The decisive error. In the Russian book on the 1948 World Championship, Keres gives some detailed analysis to show that 34 ♖dd1! leads to a draw. One plausible line is 34 ... &f7 35 ♖h1 &g6 36 ♖g1! (threatening g4) 36 ... &f7 37 ♖h1 with a draw by repetition.

34 ... h4!

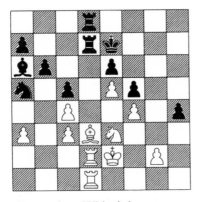

Two points. White is in *zugzwang*: any move he makes with his pieces will lead to loss of material. 35 ♖h1 loses to 35 ... ♗xc4!; 35 ♔f2 is the same, 35 ... ♗xc4!; 35 ♖c2 loses to 35 ... ♘xc4!; and of course if the knight or bishop move then the c-pawn drops again.

How would you win after 35 a4?

There is no need to change the position — 35 ... ♔f7! (one point) and White has run out of waiting moves.

| 35 | ♔e1 | |
| 35 | ... | ♘b3! |

One point. Winning material. Botvinnik makes a last ditch attempt to complicate in Reshevsky's *zeitnot* — but taking pieces off doesn't require much thought.

| 36 | ♘d5+ | |

| 36 | ... | exd5 |

One point.

| 37 | ♗xf5 | |
| 37 | ... | ♘xd2 |

One point.

| 38 | ♖xd2 | |
| 38 | ... | dxc4 |

One point. Returning some of the material is by far the simplest. A point for 38 ... ♗xc4 as well, but nothing if you tried to be greedy and moved the rook: 38 ... ♖b7 39 cxd5 and White has temporary compensation.

| 39 | ♗xd7 | |
| 39 | ... | ♖xd7 |

One point.

| 40 | ♖f2 | |
| 40 | ... | ♔e6 |

One point.

| 41 | ♖f3 | |
| 41 | ... | ♖d3 |

One point.

| 42 | ♔e2 | |

Here **White resigned**. Games such as this, where Black neutralised White's kingside attack, then went on to exploit the chronic structural weaknesses, effectively put paid to the Sämisch variation of the Nimzo in top-level chess.

16
The Spirit of Paul Morphy

Many people believe that once queens are exchanged, play tends to become dry and technical. I can't agree with that. First, the endgame can be one of the most elegant phases of the game, for when there are just a few pieces left on the board, chess is displayed in its purest form; and second, just because queens are exchanged, it doesn't mean that attacks against the king are ruled out — this game is a case in point.

The aggressor here is Yasser Seirawan, a leading American player (formerly the strongest player — before the arrival of some Soviet émigrés onto the scene). He has an uncompromising style — believing in certain kinds of positions, he is often prepared to tread a thin line in order to prove his point. To add to the pressure, he knows that in this game his opponent will probably put up an almost perfect defence: Anatoly Karpov does not lose many games at all, and indeed he very nearly survived here.

Seirawan-Karpov
Haninge 1990
English Opening
1 c4 e5 2 g3 g6 3 d4 d6 4 dxe5 dxe5 5 ♕xd8+ ♔xd8 6 ♘c3 c6

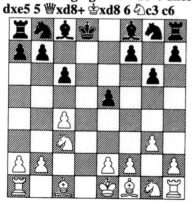

Now start trying to predict White's moves, and remember — you are up against Karpov!

7   f4

Five points. Following the queen exchange, the black king finds itself stranded in the middle of the board. White does not have a material or structural advantage, so he must try to build a quick attack against the king if he is to make anything of the position. 7 f4 is a good start: if Black captures, then the bishop reaches an excellent square on f4, preventing the king finding safety on c7; the bishop move also enables White to castle queenside, and the attack flows naturally forward. It is hardly surprising that Karpov chooses to develop a piece instead.

7   ...   ♗e6
8   ♘f3

Four points. Quick development is the key. Morphy understood it over one hundred years ago, and it is this concept which underpins most of contemporary opening theory. Thus no credit for moves such as 8 e4 or 8 fxe5.

8   ...   ♗xc4
9   ♗h3

Five points. Energetic. Seirawan continues his policy of quick development, refusing to capture the e-pawn. 9 ♘xe5 (two points) was possible, but it seems that Black may find some degree of security: 9 ... ♗e6 10 e4 ♗g7. White's pawns look impressive, but he has lost his lead in development. I'm sure this was what Karpov was hoping for when he captured on c4.

9   ...   f5

Attempting to cut the bishop from play, but making another pawn move instead of developing a piece is really asking for it.

10   b3

Five points. A finely calculated move; it requires close examination to appreciate just how strong this is:

a) If 10 ... ♗a6 11 ♘xe5. Black's

bishop is out of play on a6, and White has taken on e5 with gain of tempo; the attack plays itself: ♗b2, 0-0-0, e4 etc;

b) 10 ... ♗e6 11 ♘g5 ♔d7 12 ♗b2 with a winning attack: there are too many threats;

c) 10 ... ♗f7 11 ♘xe5 ♗e6 12 e4, and again the floodgates open. (Note how White could get a version of this last variation by capturing on e5 immediately, instead of 10 b3: 10 ♘xe5 ♗e6 11 e4. It would not be quite as good though; including 10 b3 gives White's attack an extra dimension by playing the bishop to the long diagonal. Anyhow, two points for 10 ♘xe5 and an extra one if you intended following up with 11 e4.) In view of these variations, Karpov played instead:

10   ...   ♗b4
11   ♗b2

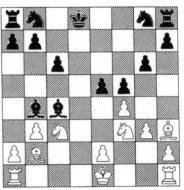

One point. Clearly the best diagonal.

11	...	&d5
12	e4	

Six points. A fantastic move, but one which meets the demands of the position. If we consider the 'natural' continuation, it will become clear how Seirawan came to find the text move.

12 0-0-0 forces Black to capture on c3: 12 ... &xc3 13 &xc3 ♘f6 14 ♘xe5 ℤf8 15 ℤhe1 ♘e4. Black has managed to secure good outposts for his minor pieces, and White's attack has been halted. On the other hand 12 e4 opens up a diagonal for the bishop on h3, for if 12 ... &xe4 13 0-0-0+ and ♘xe4 with a crushing attack; likewise if 12 ... &xc3+ 13 &xc3 &xe4 14 &xe5 &xf3 15 0-0! and White will emerge the exchange ahead.

12	...	fxe4
13	0-0-0	

Two points.

13	...	&xc3

Karpov finds the most resilient defence. If Black had played 13 ... ♘f6, how could White best continue his initiative? An extra point for 14 ♘g5, after which Black won't last long.

14	&xc3

One point.

14	...	exf3
15	&xe5	

One point.

15	...	♘d7
16	&xh8	

One point.

16	...	♘e7
17	ℤhf1	

One point. Seirawan has won the exchange, but it is still not easy to clinch victory, and here he goes slightly astray. 17 ℤhe1 (three points) was better, retaining more activity. In order to get his rook into play Black must move his king, and to do this he must first move the knight: 17 ... ♘f5 18 &d4! (to keep an eye on the f-pawn) 18 ... ♔c7 19 &xf5 gxf5 20 ℤe7 ♔d6 21 ℤxh7. Seirawan himself assesses this position as winning for White, and I suppose that with care it should be, though it is still not easy: the passed pawn on f3 protected by the superbly posted bishop are strong trumps. Black should start with 21 ... ℤe8 bringing his rook to the open file.

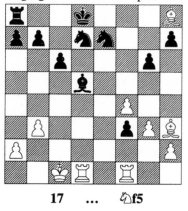

17	...	♘f5

18   ♗d4

One point. As the bishop must retreat anyway, this is the best way of dealing with the threat of 18 ... ♘e3.

18   ...   h5

19   g4

Two points. There were two ways to improve the position, this, and 19 ♗xf5 (one point) 19 ... gxf5 20 ♖de1.

19   ...   hxg4

20   ♗xg4

One point.

20   ...   ♘h4

It is not easy for White to make progress. A plan is needed.

21   ♗f2

One point.

21   ...   ♘g2

22   ♗g1

One point.

22   ...   ♘h4

23   h3

Three points.

23   ...   ♔c7

24   ♗h2

Two points. This is the point of White's manoeuvrings over the past few moves: Black's king is still slightly embarrassed, and there are possibilities to play ♗g3 menacing the knight, and thus the f-pawn.

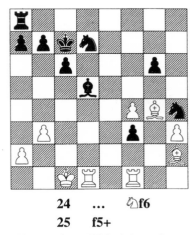

24   ...   ♘f6

25   f5+

Three points. White's best chance. If instead 25 ♗g3 ♘f5; all Black's minor pieces have found excellent posts and a way through for White is not apparent.

25   ...   ♔b6

26   fxg6

One point.

26   ...   ♘xg4

27   hxg4

One point.

27   ...   ♖g8

28   ♖d4

Three points. Seirawan has at least managed to create a passed pawn, and now he activates his pieces.

28   ...   a5

To prevent ♖b4+.

29   g5

Two points. This forces Black's knight back and gives the rook a little more room to manoeuvre.

29	...	♘xg6

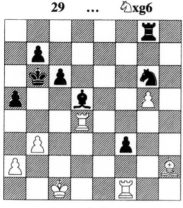

30	♔d2

Three points. An interesting idea. Seirawan wants to bring his king across the board, perhaps to take care of Black's f-pawn, but in the long term to assist the g-pawn. Marching the king up the board in the midst of Black's pieces will be difficult, but if at some opportune moment White were to sacrifice the exchange on d5 and capture the pawn on f3, it could be very promising.

30	...	♖f8
31	♗g1	

One point. Seirawan questions this move, for it allows Black's king to move back towards the middle of the board. 31 ... ♔c7! is indeed correct, with chances to draw the game. But Karpov, who now found himself in extreme time pressure after weaving a careful path through the early complications, instinctively

moved his king onto a white square (normally quite correct in view of the presence of the dark-squared bishop), but putting it even further offside, so Seirawan's gamble paid off. Objectively, it would have been better to play 31 ♗g3 (two points) but then would he have won the game?

Continuing the king march would not, for the moment, be successful: 31 ♔e3 ♖e8+ 32 ♔f2 ♖e2+.

31	...	♔a6
32	♗f2	

Two points. Securely blockading the f-pawn, and preparing to bring the rook on f1 into play.

32	...	♖f5
33	♖g4	

One point.

33	...	♘e5
34	♖g3	

One point.

34	...	♘g6
35	♖h1	

Two points. At last, White has achieved some co-ordination.

35	...	♖e5
36	♖e1	

Three points. 36 ... ♖e2 had to be prevented, and this is a useful way of doing so.

Here Karpov **lost on time**, but by now the game has turned against him anyway.

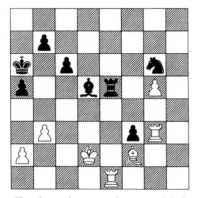

Exchanging rooks would be hopeless, so 36 ... ♖f5 37 ♖e8! with ideas of hassling Black's king, and attacking the g-pawn's blockader by ♖d8 and ♖d6. It is still a hard graft though .

The speed with which Seirawan developed an attack right from the beginning of the game was extraordinary, and rather unusual for top-level chess. It amounts to a refutation of Black's opening. If you failed to score well on the first ten moves or so, then I would strongly recommend that you study the games of Paul Morphy. He would often give up a pawn or two just to be able to achieve a lead in development, which enabled him to start a deadly attack.

17
Speed King

Vishwanathan Anand, from Madras on the south-east coast of India, is a very likely challenger for the world title in the next few years. He is already one of the strongest players in the world, and yet his style is still developing.

Anand's first international appearances were nothing short of sensational. I will never forget playing a tournament with him in 1987 in Frunze, capital of Kirghizia - one of the most far-flung outposts of the Soviet empire - when he was relatively unknown.

In one of the early rounds he faced the experienced Soviet Grandmaster Gennady Kuzmin. Anand showed as little respect for him on the chessboard as he did for anyone else, playing his moves almost instantly, even though it was an incredibly complex game, while Kuzmin brooded and sweated under increasing psychological pressure. Although Kuzmin's position had looked good early on, it gradually deteriorated, and to add to his troubles he found himself running short of time. He just managed to make the forty moves within the allotted two and a half hours, but by that stage his position was a ruin anyway. Shortly afterwards, he resigned in a total state of shock: Anand had used just fifteen minutes for all his moves.

Soviet tournaments were notorious: not only were they a severe test of one's chess ability, but also of one's endurance. Spending three weeks in a town where there is nothing to do in the evenings, where there are cockroaches in your hotel room - and probably in the unrecognisable and monotonous food that is dished up for you as well - is enough to get anyone down, yet I never saw Anand show it at all: the opposite in fact. He, and a Hungarian player, Tibor Karolyi, were the double act that kept our band of foreign players sane for the duration of the tournament. In Tamil, Anand means joy, and he could not have been given a more felicitous name .

While the speed of his play very often works in his favour, it has occasionally resulted in him making some elementary oversights. In the last couple of years he has wisely slowed down a little, and his style has broadened.

A watershed in his chess development came when he played his Candidates match against Karpov in 1991. He chose the Soviet émigré Mikhail Gurevich as his second, and his more scientific approach combined with Anand's natural gifts made a formidable team. For the first time he learned how to study properly. In the end, Karpov won the match by a narrow margin, but only after suffering a couple of shock defeats.

His opponent in this game is Ian Rogers, Australia's only grandmaster.

Anand-Rogers
Manila Interzonal 1990
French Defence

1 e4 e6 2 d4 d5 3 e5 b6 4 ♗b5+ ♗d7 5 ♗d3 c5 6 c3 ♘c6 7 ♘f3 f6 8 0-0 fxe5 9 dxe5 ♕c7 10 ♖e1 ♘h6

Start predicting White's moves now.

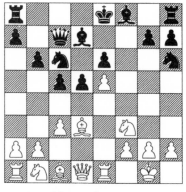

11   c4

Five points. This is a very sharp position. If White does not try to complicate then he could find that his e-pawn will be rounded up by the simple plan of ... ♘f7, ... ♗e7 and ... g5-g4. It is difficult to counter this idea when Black has such good

control of the centre thanks to the pawns on c5 and d5. 11 c4 obliges Black to push on in the centre, thus giving White the e4 square to use for a minor piece.

One point for developing moves such as 11 ♘a3, 11 ♗f4, 11 ♗xh6 and 11 ♘bd2. These are all very well, but none of them actually get to grips with the problem.

11   ...   d4

If Black had played 11 ... 0-0-0 here instead, how would you have replied?

White could take the d5 pawn: 12 cxd5 exd5 13 ♗a6+ ♔b8 14 ♕xd5, but Black gains excellent compensation after 14 ... ♘b4 15 ♕c4 ♗f5. It is much stronger to play 12 ♘c3 (two points) putting more pressure on the centre; if 12 ... d4 13 ♘b5! ♕b8 14 ♗f4, and the knight is ready to leap into d6.

12   ♘a3

Three points. The most accurate move. 12 ♗xh6 (two points) was a plausible alternative, meeting 12 ... gxh6 with 13 ♘bd2. White has more security than in the game - there is no threat of the g-pawn coming down the board to attack the knight - so consequently the e5 pawn is safer. Having said that, there are now two open files in front of White's king, so this is a gamble.

12 ... a6

13 ♗e4

Five points. Typical of Anand: he combines sound strategic moves with tricky tactics. Two points for 13 ♘c2, repositioning the knight.

13 ... 0-0-0

How would you have replied to 13 ... ♗e7 here?

14 ♗xh6 gxh6 15 b4! (two points if you found this move) was Anand's ingenious idea. If 15 ... cxb4 16 ♘b5! axb5 (if 16 ... ♕b8 then simply 17 ♘xd4) 17 cxb5. White recovers the piece and Black's position is a wreck: just compare the two pawn structures; and where can Black's king find safety?

14 ♘c2

Two points. Now that the piece sacrifice on b5 is ruled out, it is time to bring the knight to a more useful square.

14 ... ♘f7

15 ♗f4

Two points. This is a double-edged move. The e-pawn is given some more protection, but Black will be able to initiate some dangerous counterplay by attacking the bishop

with his kingside pawns.

15 b4! (five points) was more in the spirit of the position. Whichever pawn Black takes, and however it is taken, he has to open up his king, e.g. 15 ... cxb4 16 a3!, and now if Black attempts to keep the a-file closed with 16 ... b3, then 17 ♘b4!, keeps the situation fluid; or alternatively, 15 ... ♘cxe5 16 ♘xe5 ♘xe5 17 ♗f4 ♗d6 18 bxc5 bxc5 19 ♗xe5 ♗xe5 20 ♖b1 with a blistering attack.

In these variations it is not worth counting pawns too much: the most important thing is to open up lines towards Black's king; it has no close pawn cover so it is potentially in a perilous state.

15 ... ♗e7

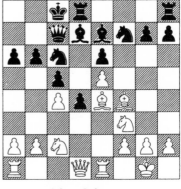

16 b4

Three points. For other moves, no points. It is essential that White creates some play on the queenside.

16 ... g5

17   &g3

One point.

17   ...   g4

It probably would have been better for Black to play 17 ... h5 hassling the bishop.

18   &d2

One point. 18 &h4, putting the knight out of play at the edge of the board, barely comes into consideration.

18   ...   &cxe5

Anand must have been very glad to see this move. For the cost of just one pawn the bishop on g3 has been brought back to life.

19   a4

Four points. An energetic move. Anand is striving at all costs to open up lines on the queenside. It was also possible to play more safely with 19 bxc5 (two points) and if 19 ... &xc5 20 &b3, keeping up the pressure.

19   ...   cxb4

20   a5

One point. Otherwise 19 a4 has no point.

20   ...   bxa5

21   &xd4

Two points. This is good, but if you are getting into the swing of this game then you would surely have realised that it was time to sacrifice pawn number four.

21 c5! (five points) is devastating.

If the pawn is taken, 21 ... &xc5 22 &c4 is decisive; Black has no satisfactory way out of the pins and discovered attacks — check it yourself. It is better to stop the knight coming into c4 with 21 ... &b5, but then 22 &b3 and if 22 ... a4 23 &xb4! axb3 24 &xa6! &xa6 25 &xa6, with a crushing attack.

These are just a couple of sample variations, but it is quite clear which way the traffic is heading. Notice how White, by sacrificing material, has managed to seize the initiative so that all the action is concentrated on the queenside — his king is never in danger in any of these lines.

21   ...   &c5

22   &4b3

Two points. There was a clear choice between this and 22 &2b3. However, 22 &2b3 runs into 22 ... a4 23 &xc5 &xc5. Before doing anything else, White will have to escape from the pin on the d-file.

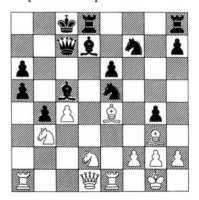

22	...	a4
23	♘xc5	

One point.

23	...	♕xc5
24	♗c2	

Four points. This is a difficult move to find: it hardly seems logical to remove the bishop from such a wonderful diagonal, but it is absolutely necessary to break through to Black's king.

There was an even more brutal method of doing this at White's disposal: 24 ♖xa4 (two points). I doubt whether it is sound - a rook is a bit too much to invest - but in a proper game it would be difficult for Black to defend himself: 24 ... ♗xa4 25 ♕xa4 ♖xd2 26 ♕xa6+, and the fun begins.

24	...	a5

This is hardly the most testing defence, though I can imagine that by this stage Black was in a state of shock — or perhaps he just considered that his position was lost.

24 ... b3 was the most obvious move, but this runs into ... ?

25 ♗xb3! (one point) 25 ... axb3 26 ♘xb3, and the attack flows on. Although a piece down, White must be winning this position: every single piece is contributing to the struggle. A plausible continuation might run: 26 ... ♕c7 (to keep the knight on e5 protected) 27 ♖xa6 ♗c6 28 ♕a1

♗b7 29 ♖a5. Black's last hope, ... ♕c6, is prevented, and the knight on e5 is about to drop.

25	♘e4	

Two points. Deduct five if you were so careless as to play 25 ♗xa4 ♗xa4 26 ♕xa4 ♖xd2, losing a piece.

25	...	♕c7
26	♗xa4	

One point.

26	...	♗c6
27	♕c2	

Two points. The best square. If 27 ♕e2 ♗xa4 28 ♖xa4 ♕xc4 is irritating; and 27 ♕b3 is met by 27 ... ♖d3.

27	...	♗b7
28	c5	

Three points. The clearest continuation. Black is already in an awful mess with the pin on e5, and this sets up all kinds of nasty threats along side it: perhaps c6; maybe ♘d6+ — something is bound to work for White.

28	...	♖d5

Instead of this, what would you have played in reply to 28...♔b8?

Putting both king and queen in the line of the bishop on g3 looks like suicide — and it is. A bonus point if you found 29 ♘g5 exploiting this situation.

29	♗b3	

One point and the same for 29
♖ac1.

29   ...   ♖hd8

30   ♖ac1

Three points. Nothing for 30 ♗xd5.
The rook is not running away (e6
and indirectly e5 hang) so why take
it? After 30 ... ♖xd5 31 ♖ac1 ♛c6!
Black is able to establish some kind
of blockade. Compare this with the
game.

30   ...   ♛c6

31   ♗a4

Two points. One of the reasons for
keeping the bishop.

31   ...   ♛c7

32   ♘d6+

Three points. From here it is
possible to calculate right through
to the finish.

32   ...   ♖8xd6

If 32 ... ♘fxd6 33 cxd6 ♛xc2 34
♖xc2+ ♔b8 35 ♗xe5 wins a piece.

33   cxd6

One point.

33   ...   ♛xc2

34   ♖xc2+

One point.

34   ...   ♔b8

35   ♗b3

One point.

35   ...   ♖xd6

36   ♖xe5

Three points. A clean finish; if 36
... ♖d1+ 37 ♖e1+. Here **Black
resigned**. Although not perfect - he
plays too quickly for that - this was
a sparkling performance from
Anand.

18
Genius

The variety, and number, of tributes to Mikhail Tal which followed his death in 1992 was a mark of the esteem and affection that he was held in by chessplayers around the world. He touched everyone whom he met with his great spirit, kindness, mischievous humour, and his passion and genius for chess.

I was lucky enough to play in a couple of tournaments with him, the first one on his home territory in Jurmala, near Riga, in 1985. Jurmala is a pleasant coastal resort; the air is good and there is a nice beach. It was coming to the end of the summer and the rush of tourists was over. For much of the tournament Tal just cruised along, not giving the chess his all; instead he was enjoying relaxing with his wife and young daughter. He would agree short draws with the stronger players, then pick off the weakies when it suited him.

Nevertheless, by the end he could still share first place if he won his last round game. His opponent, the Danish International Master Carsten Høi, would be no push-over — he had already beaten the solid Soviet GM Vladimir Tukmakov, and the eccentric Latvian master Alvis Vitolinsh.

But on this day, Høi didn't stand a chance. Tal was gunning for him. His attitude at the board was one of intense concentration. I remember watching Tal while he lit up a cigarette, sucking in the nicotine as though it were his life-blood, but never averting his gaze from the chessboard through the whole operation. In the time it took me to stroll to the side of the stage and back again, all that was left of the cigarette was a column of ash that had dropped onto the table, and the merest wisp of smoke coming from Tal's nostrils.

Tal-Høi
Jurmala 1985
Pirc Defence

1 e4 g6 2 d4 ♗g7 3 c3 d6 4 ♘f3
♘f6 5 ♗d3 0-0 6 0-0 ♘c6 7 ♗g5 h6 8 ♗h4 ♘h5

Now try and predict White's moves.

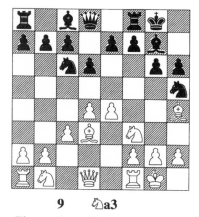

9   ♘a3

Five points. How many of you chose the stereotyped 9 ♘bd2 (two points) here? Why Tal developed the knight to this abstruse square will become apparent later.

Nothing for 9 d5 — not a very beautiful move, giving away control of the e5 square. Black may play 9 ... ♘b8; or 9 ... ♘e5! 10 ♘xe5 dxe5, followed by ... ♘f4, ... g5 and ... e6. Black stands well.

9   ...   ♘f4
10   ♗c2

Two points. It is essential to keep this bishop, so no points if you left it on d3 to be taken. This is one of White's strongest attacking pieces!

One point for both 10 ♗b5 and 10 ♗c4.

10   ...   ♗g4
11   ♕d2

Three points. Now it is clear why the knight went to a3 and not d2: Tal had foreseen that the knight was coming to f4, and wanted to evict it from this ideal outpost straight away.

One point for 11 h3 breaking the pin. However, Black then seizes the initiative after 11 ... ♗xf3 12 ♕xf3 g5! 13 ♗g3 e5!. Nothing for 11 ♗g3 e5!. I imagine White will eventually be reduced to exchanging the knight off for the bishop, but then he will have no chance for the advantage.

11   ...   g5

Before going on to consider your response to this move, what would you have played in reply to 11 ... ♗xf3 here?

12 ♕xf4! was correct (not 12 gxf3 g5 13 ♗g3 e5 or 13 ... ♘g6! with an excellent position). And now 12 ... ♗e2 13 ♖fe1 ♗a6 14 ♕e3 g5 15 ♗g3 e5 16 ♖ad1 is the most likely continuation. A strange position has arisen: everything is 'normal', as the Russians like to say, bar those two odd-looking minor pieces on the a-file. Take another three points depending on how much you saw.

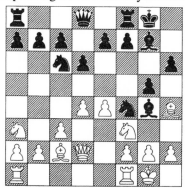

12   ♘xg5!

Five points. Tal did not make sacrifices just for the sake of it (well, only occasionally), but as and when the position demanded it. Here he realised that retreating the bishop would leave him with a clearly inferior position: 12 ♗g3 ♗xf3! 13 ♗xf4 (13 gxf3 e5 or 13 ... ♘g6, as in a previous note) 13 ... gxf4 14 gxf3 e5! 15 d5 ♘e7. Black is ready to launch a serious assault on the kingside beginning with ... ♘e7-g6-h4 — and what is that knight doing on a3?

So the sacrifice was necessary. Not that this was a spur of the moment decision — I imagine he saw the rough outlines of the idea when playing 9 ♘a3. If you saw this sacrifice coming, at least before 11 ♕d2, then take another couple of points.

12 ♗xg5 is not so good: 12 ... hxg5 13 ♘xg5 e5! and Black does not have to retreat the knight.

12   ...   hxg5

Did you consider 12 ... ♘g6? If not, do so now!

White has some tempting possibilities:

a) Two points for 13 ♗g3 hxg5 14 ♕xg5 ♗d7 15 f4 with a strong attack;

b) Unfortunately 13 ♘xf7 isn't terribly good, not because of 13 ... ♖xf7 14 ♗b3! ♘xh4 15 ♗xf7+ ♔xf7 16 ♕f4+ ♔g8 17 ♕xg4, when Black

will get steam-rollered by White's pawns; but instead, 13 ... ♔xf7! (remember this idea from game 11, Adams-Shirov?) 14 ♗b3 + ♔e8 15 ♗g3 e5, and Black should survive;

c) I think the best move is 13 ♗b3! (three points). If 13 ... hxg5 14 ♗xg5 with a similar attack to the game; and if 13 ... e6 14 ♘xe6! ♕xh4 15 ♘xf8 ♖xf8 16 f4, and again, White's pawn-roller makes up for the slight material disadvantage of bishop and knight versus rook.

13   ♗xg5

One point.

13   ...   ♘g6
14   f4!

Two points. It is important to keep Black on the defensive. White threatens to play f5, driving the knight from g6 and trapping the bishop on g4.

14   ...   f6
15   f5!

Two points. This had to be foreseen before playing 14 f4 — an extra two points if you did so. If now 15 ... fxg5 16 ♗b3+! (16 fxg6?? e6 throws away everything) 16 ... ♔h7 17 ♕xg5, regaining one of the pieces with a crushing attack. Two more points if you accurately calculated this variation.

15   ...   e6

If 15 ... ♘h8, you play ... ?

16 ♗b3+! ♔h7 (16 ... ♘f7 17 ♗e3 and the bishop on g4 is trapped) 17 ♗e3 followed by ♖f4-h4 with a mating attack. Another point if you saw this.

16   ♗h6

Two points for this and 16 ♗e3 which also gives White a very strong attack: 16 ... exf5 17 exf5 ♘ge7 18 ♕f2!. It is difficult for Black to bring his pieces over to defend the kingside. Deduct five for 16 fxg6?? fxg5, when Black is close to consolidating his extra piece, particularly as I mentioned it on the previous note.

16   ...   exf5

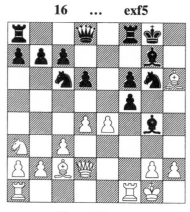

17   h3!

Three points. It would not be so good to play 17 exf5 (only one point) in this case. The exchange of the bishop on g7 will ease Black's cramped position, giving him greater chances to defend than in the note to White's 16th move where the bishop

stood on e3.

17   ...   f4!?

An interesting idea. Since he is going to lose the piece back anyway, Black just leaves it en prise, but thinks that this way he might be able to close the kingside. (Of course 17 ... ♗h5 was out of the question: 18 ♖xf5.)

18   ♗xg7

One point.

18   ...   ♔xg7
19   hxg4

One point.

19   ...   ♖h8

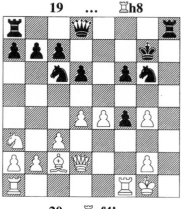

20   ♖xf4!

Five points. This, along with 9 ♘a3, is the hardest move of the game to find. Having just regained his material - White is even a pawn up - Tal sacrifices again. Was it necessary? In this case, not strictly, it is more a matter of style.

It was possible to try and

consolidate the extra pawn with 20 ♗d1!?♖h4 21 ♗f3 ♕h8 22 ♔f2 ♖h2 23 ♔e2 intending ♔d3-c2, before getting going on Black's king. Two points if you had envisaged this king march. Such tortuous stuff is not to Tal's taste though, he much prefers to seize the initiative.

>   20   ...   ♘xf4
>   21   ♕xf4

One point.

>   21   ...   ♖h6
>   22   ♔f2

Two points. Anticipating ... ♕h8. Anyway, White's king is safer behind the mass of pawns in the centre.

>   22   ...   ♘e5?

This move rather spoils the game. With two pawns for the exchange and such a strong centre, White undoubtedly has the better chances, but the win is a long way off. Black's best move was 22 ... ♘e7, bolstering the kingside. In particular, it is very important to cover f5: White is finally threatening to glide the knight into the game - ♘a3-c4-e3-f5 - with lethal effect.

22 ... ♘e5 was a panic reaction brought on by time trouble. That is one way of explaining it. It is curious how Tal always seemed to be 'lucky'. With uncanny consistency he managed to provoke unforced errors from his opponents. (There is the famous story of how Pal Benkö

wore dark glasses when playing him to ward off the famous Tal stare, rumoured to hypnotise his opponents into blundering.)

But the real secret is to be found in the nature of his play — 20 ♖xf4 in this game is an excellent example. After the initial sacrifice on g5, he has not given his opponent a moment's breathing space. Instead of relaxing on the 20th move, he instinctively knew that it was correct to keep the pressure up by sacrificing once more. It was this constant setting of fresh problems that his opponents found difficult to cope with.

>   23   dxe5

One point. Why not?

>   23   ...   fxe5
>   24   ♕g3

Two points. The best, stopping the most unpleasant check on h4.

>   24   ...   ♕g5

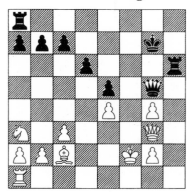

25   ♘c4!

Three points. This is the decisive move in the game. Once the knight centralises Black is finished.

25   ...   ♖f8+
26   ♔e2

One point.

26   ...   ♖f4
27   ♘e3!

One point.

27   ...   ♔f8
28   ♖f1

Two points. Exchanging Black's active pieces is the simplest way to proceed.

28   ...   ♔e8
29   ♖f3

Two points.

29   ...   ♖h1
30   ♕f2

One point.

30   ...   ♖a1
31   ♗b3

One point.

31   ...   ♖b1
32   ♔d3

One point.

32   ...   c6
33   g3

Two points. This is what White has been building up to playing for the last few moves. If now 33 ... ♖xf3 34 ♕xf3 ♖xb2 35 ♕f7+ ♔d8

36 ♕xb7 is carnage.

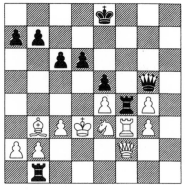

33   ...   ♖xb2
34   gxf4

One point. The ending is winning easily. Deduct three if you played 34 ♕xb2 ♖xf3 35 ♕e2 ♖xg3. White can even lose this position.

34   ...   ♖xf2
35   fxg5

One point.

35   ...   ♖xf3
36   ♔e2

No points for this. Tal's technique is a little lax. 36 g6 (one point) was the simplest.

36   ...   ♖f4
37   ♔d3

One point.

37   ...   ♔f8
38   g6

One point.

38   ...   ♖f3

39   &♗f7

One point.

39   ...   **b5**

40   &♔e2

Two points.

40   ...   ♖f4

41   ♘f5

Two points.

41   ...   ♖xe4+

If instead 41 ... ♖xg4, not 42 g7+ ♔xf7 43 ♘h6+ ♔xg7 44 ♘xg4 ♔f7 which is very difficult to win; but simply 42 ♘xd6.

42   ♔f3

One point.

42   ...   ♖f4+

43   ♔g3

One point. **Black resigned**. There is no defence to 43 ♗e6 and g7+.

19
Master v. Pupil

This game is a fascinating clash of styles. Judit Polgar is the youngest and strongest of the three sisters from Budapest. In 1992 she beat Bobby Fischer's record to become the youngest-ever Grandmaster and is now one of the top thirty or so rated players in the world. She has a sharp, dynamic style of play, always ready to attack no matter who her opponent is. Judit has built an opening repertoire that fits perfectly with this: 1 e4 as White, and Sicilians and King's Indians as Black. Her opponent, Alexander Chernin, is a Russian grandmaster who, ironically, has recently moved to Hungary in order to train the Polgar sisters. He has a reputation of being one of the most solid players on the tournament circuit, though it should be said that in this game he plays very ambitiously indeed.

Chernin-J. Polgar
New Delhi 1990
King's Indian Defence

1 c4 g6 2 d4 ♘f6 3 ♘c3 ♗g7 4 e4 d6 5 h3 0-0 6 ♘f3 e5 7 d5 ♘a6 8 ♗e3 ♘h5 9 ♘h2

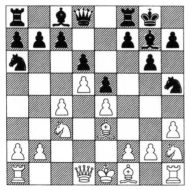

Try predicting Black's moves now.

9 ... ♕e8

Five points. Black is trying to play ... f5, but if she does so immediately then 9 ... f5 10 exf5, and now 10 ... ♗xf5 fails to 11 g4, and 10... gxf5 leaves the knight on h5 hanging. Now we can see the point of 9 ... ♕e8 — it would protect the knight in this last variation.

9 ... ♘f4 looks logical, again with the idea of ... f5, but White can play 10 g3 ♘xh3 11 ♘f3, winning the knight.

10 ♗e2
10 ... f5

Four points. Judit can't be bothered

messing around any longer; she prefers to break out immediately — even though it costs a pawn.

10 ... ♘f4 (four points) was just as good, it is really a matter of taste. Play might continue 11 ♗f3 f5 with great complications. Kasparov once won a spectacular game against Kavalek playing in this way, although improvements were later found for White, which is no doubt why Chernin was willing to repeat the opening.

11 exf5

11 ♗xh5 would not be advisable. The slight structural damage which Black incurs is more than compensated for by the possession of the two bishops, and the open g-file.

11 ... ♘f4

Three points. The only follow-up. 11 ... gxf5 leaves the knight on h5 *en prise*.

12 ♗xf4

12 ... exf4

One point.

13 fxg6

13 ... ♕xg6

One point.

14 ♔f1

If I were White, I would have thought twice before taking this pawn. Black has superb compensation: the two bishops have far-ranging perspectives; the queen

stands on an excellent square; White has been unable to castle, so his forces are disconnected. I suppose it is a matter of style: Chernin likes defending — he would have to with this position.

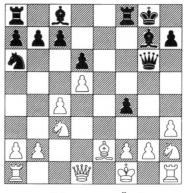

14 ... ♘c5

Three points. Bringing the knight into play.

15 ♖c1

15 ... ♗f5

Two points.

16 ♘f3

16 ... ♗f6

Four points. It was vital to prevent 17 ♘h4. If for instance 16 ... ♖ae8 17 ♘h4! ♕g5 18 ♘xf5 ♖xf5 19 ♗f3, and with g2 securely protected it will be very difficult to crack White's fortress.

17 ♔g1

17 ... ♔h8

Four points. Attacking down the g-file is the clearest way to continue, but Black has good alternatives: 17 … ♖ae8 (two points) is a sensible developing move, and although 17 … ♘d3 (one point) forces White to give up his bishop (18 ♗xd3 ♗xd3 19 b3), exchanging pieces eases the defender's task.

18 ♔h2

18 … ♖g8

One point.

19 ♖g1

19 … ♕h6

Three points. Apart from anything else, White might have been contemplating 20 g4, so this is sensible.

20 ♗f1

20 … ♖g7

Two points.

21 b4

21 … ♘d7

One point. If White now played 22 ♘d4, how would you reply?

Unfortunately 22 … ♗xh3 isn't very effective: 23 gxh3 ♖xg1 24 ♔xg1 ♕g7+ 25 ♕g4 ♗xd4 26 ♘b5, and the situation has cleared to White's advantage. 22 … ♗xd4 23 ♕xd4 ♘e5 is correct (two points if you found both these moves) with all kinds of nasty threats in the air: 24 … ♗xh3 25 gxh3 ♘f3+ 26 ♔h1 ♘xg1 is the most obvious.

22 ♗d3

White tries to eliminate the troublesome light-squared bishop.

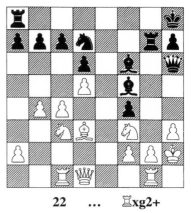

22 … ♖xg2+

Seven points. Chernin must have been seduced into thinking that the worst was over, for if the bishops are exchanged, as seems forced, then Black's attack loses much of its force. Judit's sacrifice is decisive.

23 ♖xg2

23 … ♗xh3

One point.

24 ♘e4

If White had played 24 ♔g1, how would you have replied (more than one move is involved)?

24 … ♗xg2 25 ♔xg2 ♗xc3! (better than 25 … ♕g7+, as Black keeps the option of … ♖g8+). Black has won a pawn and maintains the attack; two points if you found this.

24 … ♘e5!

Six points. This is probably the move that Chernin overlooked: it is very difficult to see such a follow-up when one would be expecting a lethal discovered check.

Nothing for 24 ... ♗xg2+ 25 ♔xg2 ♖g8+ 26 ♔f1 ♕h3+ 27 ♔e2 when White's king has found security.

25 ♘xe5

If White had played 25 ♘xf6, how would you respond (a variation is required)?

The simplest way to win is 25 ... ♗g4+ 26 ♔g1 ♘xf3+ 27 ♔f1 ♕h1+ 28 ♔e2 ♘d4+ 29 ♔d2 ♗xd1. Three points if you found all of this; a long variation, but White had no sensible alternatives en route, so it wasn't too difficult.

25 ... ♗xe5

Two points. Deduct as many as you think fit for 25 ... ♗g4+, which if brought to its logical conclusion ends in 26 ♔g1 ♗xd1 27 ♘f7 mate.

26 ♘g5

White had two major alternatives. How would you have replied to a) 26 ♔g1; b) 26 f3 instead?

a) 26 ♔g1 ♗xg2 27 ♔xg2 ♖g8+ 28 ♔f1 f3! and to avoid mate White must play 29 ♕xf3, allowing 29 ... ♕xc1+ with a simple win — three points for all this;

b) 26 f3 ♗xg2+ 27 ♔xg2 ♖g8+ 28 ♔f1 ♕h1+ 29 ♔e2 ♖g2+ 30 ♘f2 ♖xf2+ 31 ♔xf2 ♘d4+ 32 ♔e2 ♕g2+ 33 ♔e1 ♕f2 mate. Another three points for this. Once again, these are long variations, but as they are forcing, I don't think they are particularly difficult to find.

26 ... ♗xg2+

One point.

27 ♔xg2

27 ... ♕xg5+

One point.

28 ♔f3

Into the unknown. It occurs to me that if White were able to swap his king and queen around in this position, then he would not stand at all badly.

28 ... ♖g8

Three points. The simplest. 28 ... ♕h5+ is fun — it forces 29 ♔e4, but I don't see a way to win here. If for instance 29 ... f3 30 ♕xf3 ♕h4+ 31 ♔e3 ♕g5+ 32 ♔e2 ♕xc1 33 ♕h5 is more than irritating. So, no points.

29 ♔e2

29 ... f3+

Three points.

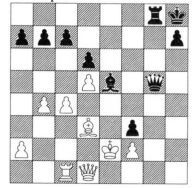

Here **White resigned** in view of 30 ♔e1 ♗f4!. A deft blow. Among others, the threat is 31 ... ♖e8+, and if 31 ♕xf3 then 31 ... ♗xc1.

20
A Life of Struggle

Viktor Korchnoi is one of my favourite players. When going over his games one always gains the impression that he is striving at all costs to win. In positions which on the surface appear dry, he will summon all his creative energies to find a way to unbalance the play, even risking losing by doing so — though more often than not he will manage to outwit his opponent in the complications.

Korchnoi was part of that great generation of players which emerged in the Soviet Union in the 1950s. It has been suggested that these players owed their strength and fighting spirit on the chessboard to the fact that they all somehow managed to survive the horrors and privations of Stalin's regime and the 'Great Patriotic War' (World War II). Bismarck's saying, 'That which does not destroy me makes me stronger', springs to mind.

It is certainly true that conflict and struggle have dominated Korchnoi's life, and that he actually seems to thrive on it: on the chessboard and off it.

In his autobiography, *Chess is my Life* (Batsford, 1977) Korchnoi writes: 'Chessplayers are of varying character. Some, in order to be confident of success, have to see their opponents as a friend, while others must, without fail, feel enmity towards the opponent ... There are many more of the second type, and it must be admitted that the author belongs to this group.'

One only needs to think of his bitter rivalry with Anatoly Karpov to realise how well Korchnoi knows himself. Naturally, a great deal of this had to do with Korchnoi's defection in 1976 and Karpov's privileged position within the Soviet Union — though by all accounts their relations could hardly be described as cordial even before then.

Korchnoi's defection actually gave him a new lease of life — his playing strength improved dramatically in the following couple of years, and the game below is from that time. This year (1993) he celebrates his 62nd birthday, and though he does not enjoy the same consistency of results as ten years ago, he is still capable of matching the very best in the world. His struggle against Kasparov in the 1992 European Team Championships, in which the World Champion had to call upon all his reserves in order to avoid defeat - the game ended in a draw - attests to his great powers.

Korchnoi's opponent here is Grandmaster Eugenio Torre from the Philippines, at that time one of the strongest players in Asia.

Torre-Korchnoi
Buenos Aires 1978
Caro-Kann Defence

1 e4 c6 2 d4 d5 3 ♘c3 dxe4 4 ♘xe4 ♘f6 5 ♘xf6+ exf6 6 ♘f3 ♗d6 7 ♗e2 ♘a6 8 0-0 ♘c7 9 c4 0-0 10 ♗e3

Now start predicting Black's moves.

10 ... ♖e8

Four points. Lining up the rook opposite the bishops makes good sense. At the moment there is no threat, but one never knows when the situation could be exploited tactically.

Two points for 10 ... ♗e6, 10 ... ♗f5 or 10 ... ♗g4. All these moves

are reasonable, but it is not yet clear what the best square for the bishop will be — another advantage of playing the rook first.

11 ♕d2

11 ... ♗f5

Two points. This is the best diagonal for the bishop — but I didn't want to give the game away on the last move! One point for 11 ... ♗g4 and 11 ... ♗e6.

12 ♖ad1

12 ... ♗e4

Three points. It is curious that it is Black who is the more aggressively placed, even though White, with two strong centre pawns, ought to be controlling the play. We can clearly see the advantages of the doubled f-pawns: the central files were opened enabling Black to develop freely and even establish some control over the e-file; and the f-pawn, which would normally find itself on e6 in the Caro-Kann, prevents White's knight from occupying its traditional outpost on e5.

One point for 12 ... ♕d7 connecting the rooks — a sensible continuation.

13 ♕c1

13   ...   h6

Three points. Don't be fooled by this modest move, Korchnoi is actually plotting something evil.

Two points for the provocative and enterprising 13 ... ♘e6. Black is ideally placed to meet 14 d5 — 14 ... cxd5 15 cxd5 ♖c8!; and might try to play the knight into f4 (prepared by ... ♛c7).

One point for the solid but now uninspired 13 ... ♛d7. Incidentally, Black need never fear White playing c5, which simply cedes the d5 square.

14   ♘d2
14   ...   ♗h7

One point. The bishop had to be preserved, and tucking it right out of the way in the corner is the best.

15   ♗f3
15   ...   f5

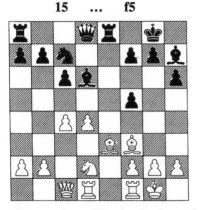

Four points. The beginning of Korchnoi's grand plan. Because he

has a spare f-pawn, he is able to throw it up the board without fearing that his king will become exposed.

16   ♘b3
16   ...   g5

Six points. This is the star move of the game. Now we can see why Korchnoi played 13 ... h6: the bishop could well have dropped back to g6 or f5 without anything untoward occurring, but clearing it right out of the way enabled him to throw his kingside pawns forward. Their advance highlights the poor position of White's bishops which have looked distinctly wooden since the start of the game.

If White now played 17 g3, how would you reply?

17 ... ♛f6 (one point) is correct: the queen takes up an attacking position (... f4 is now threatened), and at the same time lends the king some protection.

17   ♘a5
17   ...   g4

Two points. This is the beginning of some far-sighted calculation. I can think of many players who would think for thirty seconds and then play the obvious 17 ... ♖b8 (have a point if you did). Korchnoi has sensed that he can win material and is prepared to tread a narrow path to do so.

18   ♗e2

What would you have played in

reply to 18 ♘xb7?

Two points if you found 18 ... ♗xh2+ 19 ♔xh2 ♕h4+ 20 ♔g1 gxf3 with a lethal attack: if 21 gxf3 ♔h8 and ... ♖g8+.

18 ... ♗b4

Five points. It looks unnatural to remove the bishop from an attacking diagonal, so this is a hard move to find.

19 ♘xb7

It was also necessary to consider the consequences of 19 ♘b3. At first glance it looks as though Black wins a piece with the simple 19 ... f4. However after 20 ♗d2! matters are not so clear (if 20 ... ♖xe2 21 ♗xb4, and Black's kingside pawn push is beginning to look decidedly rash). However, Black can still win with 20 ... f3! 21 gxf3 ♗d6 22 ♖fe1 gxf3 23 ♗xf3 ♕h4, with a deadly attack.

Remember, Korchnoi would have had to have found all this before playing 17 ... g4. No wonder he runs short of time so often ...

19 ... ♕c8

One point.

20 ♘c5

If 20 ♗xh6 ♖xe2 21 ♕g5+ ♗g6 22 ♕f6 ♗f8, or 22 ... ♘e8, saves and wins.

20 ... f4

Two points. This is the point of Black's previous play — he wins a

piece by force.

21 ♗xg4

21 ... ♕xg4

One point.

22 ♗xf4

Black has won a piece but must play with extreme caution: his king is slightly exposed and he doesn't have too many pawns left. What rescues him is the fact that his pieces are so active.

22 ... ♘e6

One point. There was no sense in protecting the beast. If now 23 ♘xe6 ♖xe6, Black's rook is ready to swing across to g6; and on 23 ♗xh6 ♘xd4 is excellent.

23 ♗e3

23 ... ♖ad8

Two points. The most active; Black's last piece comes into play. Deduct two if you played 23 ... h5: a just punishment for such materialism.

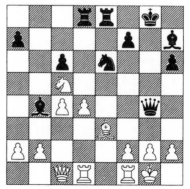

24	♘d3
24	... ♗d6

Two points. Returning to the best diagonal. Take a look at Black's pieces: they are superbly co-ordinated.

Deduct two if you played 23 ... ♗xd3 exchanging off one of your fabulous bishops. It does not win a pawn: 24 ♖xd3 ♘xd4 25 ♗xd4 ♖xd4 26 ♖g3.

25	♘e5
25	... ♗xe5

Two points.

26	dxe5
26	... ♗d3

Two points. Black wins a pawn and exchanges the queens by force (in this case it's okay to give up a bishop) for if 26 ♖fe1 then 26 ... ♗e4 leads to checkmate.

27	f3
27	... ♕xc4

One point.

28	♕xc4
28	... ♗xc4

One point.

29	♖xd8
29	... ♘xd8

Two points. The most accurate move. If 29 ... ♖xd8 30 ♖c1 ♗xa2 31 ♖xc6, and Black still has two pawns *en prise*.

30	♖d1

30	... ♗xa2

One point.

31	♗xa7
31	... ♗d5

Four points. It is difficult to imagine too much going wrong with Black's position while the bishop is cemented to this square.

32	f4

Korchnoi must have been glad to see this move: he undoubtedly has a winning position but lengthening the diagonal of the bishop makes it much easier to bring the game to a conclusion.

32	... ♘e6

Three points. Bringing the knight back into play. If 33 f5 ♘f4 34 g3 ♘h3+ 35 ♔f1 ♖xe5 wins a pawn.

33	♗e3
33	... h5

Two points. Establishing control over the white squares on the kingside. Once White's pawns are immobilised then they can be attacked. If 34 f5 ♘g7 35 f6 ♘e6 doesn't help White at all.

34	h3
34	... ♖b8

One point.

35	♖d2
35	... ♖b3

Two points. Korchnoi continues to play with great energy. In the space of just a few moves, White has been put onto the defensive.

36   &f2

36   ...   h4

Three points. Fixing the kingside pawns.

37   &c2

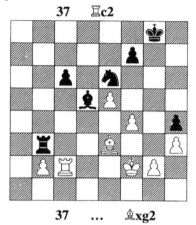

37   ...   &xg2

Three points. Winning back another pawn. Incidentally, this would not have been quite so good on the previous turn when White could have played 36 ... &xg2 37 f5! and then brought the rook down to the eighth rank, causing some confusion.

If you played the elegant 37 ... &g7 with the idea ... &f5 improving Black's bind on the position, then also take two points.

Anyway, **White resigned** here, which perhaps supports the argument for Korchnoi's brutality over elegance. There are not many players who would conceive of the idea to throw their pawns up in front of their own king, but Korchnoi must have had this in mind from a very early stage. The most difficult phase of the game was probably when Black won the piece: in some ways these moves were 'illogical' - 18 ... &b4 did not fit in with the flow of the game - but were based on precise calculation: one of Korchnoi's great strengths.